THE LIFE OF MAN

a time to weep...
and a
time to laugh

THE LIFE OF MAN

a time to weep... and a time to laugh

By the Editors of Country Beautiful

Publisher & Editorial Director: Michael P. Dineen
Executive Editor: Robert L. Polley
Edited by Caroline Poh

Country Beautiful
Waukesha, Wisconsin

Clemens Kalischer

Clemens Kalischer

COUNTRY BEAUTIFUL: *Publisher and Editorial Director:* Michael P. Dineen; *Executive Editor:* Robert L. Polley; *Senior Editors:* Kenneth L. Schmitz, James H. Robb; *Art Director:* Buford Nixon; *Managing Editor:* John M. Nuhn; *Contributing Editor:* Caroline Poh; *Associate Editors:* D'Arlyn Marks, Kay Kundinger; *Editorial Assistant:* Nancy Backes; *Production Manager:* Donna Griesemer; *Administration:* Brett E. Gries, Bruce Schneider; *Administrative Secretary:* Kathleen M. Stoner.

Country Beautiful Corporation is a wholly owned subsidiary of Flick-Reedy Corporation: *President:* Frank Flick; *Vice President and General Manager:* Michael P. Dineen; *Treasurer and Secretary:* August Caamano.

ACKNOWLEDGEMENTS

The editors are grateful to the following publishers, authors, and copyright holders for permission to use the following copyright material in this volume:

Excerpt from *New Hopes For A Changing World* by Bertrand Russell reprinted by permission of George Allen & Unwin Ltd.

Excerpt from *Sunset and Twilight* by Bernard Berenson reprinted by permission of Baron Dr. Cecil Anrep.

"The Ancient Beautiful Things" by Fannie Stearns Davis reprinted by permission of *The Atlantic Monthly.*

Excerpt from "Each Night a Child Is Born" by Sophia Lyon Fahs by permission of Dorothy Fahs Beck.

Excerpt from *Duties of The Heart* by Bahya Ibn Pakuda reprinted by permission of Boys Town Jerusalem Press.

"Four" by Elise Gibbs, reprinted by permission of *The Saturday Evening Post,* © 1955 The Curtis Publishing Company.

Selection by Theocritus of Syracuse from *Greek Poetry for Everyman,* translated by F. L. Lucas, reprinted by permission of J. M. Dent & Sons, Ltd.

"Bright Journey," Orange Birds" and "Road's End" from the book *The Dark Cavalier: The Collected Poems of Margaret Widdemer,* © 1958 by Margaret Widdemer; "Youth" by Theresa Helburn, from *Girl Scout Stories, Second Book* edited by H. J. Ferris, © 1926 by Girl Scouts, Inc.; "Age Invading" by Aline Kilmer, © 1919 by George H. Doran Company; and excerpt from *The Almost Perfect State* by Don Marquis; reprinted by permission of Doubleday & Company, Inc.

"Such a Little Child" by Dorothy Ashny Pownall, © 1936 Downe Publishing, Inc., reprinted by permission of *Ladies' Home Journal.*

Excerpt from *The House at Pooh Corner* by A. A. Milne, copyright, © 1928 by E. P. Dutton & Co., Inc. Renewal, 1958, by A. A. Milne. Published by E. P. Dutton & Co., Inc. and used with their permission.

"The Children of Berlin," "The Enemy," and excerpt from "Homecoming" by Ethel Boehm Foth.

Excerpt from "Blessings on Little Boys" by Arthur Guiterman from *Death and General Putnam,* Dutton,© 1935, renewed by Vida Lindo Guiterman. Reprinted by permission of Vida Lindo Guiterman.

Excerpts from *Wind, Sand and Stars* by Antoine de Saint Exupery; excerpts from "The Cracked Looking Glass" from *Flowering Judas and Other Stories* by Katherine Anne Porter; and "in Just-" and "from spiralling ecstatically this" by E. E. Cummings reprinted by permission of Harcourt Brace Jovanivich, Inc.

Excerpt from "Threnody for a Brown Girl" from *On These I Stand* by Countee Cullen reprinted by permission of Harper & Row, Publishers, Inc.

Excerpt from *An Anthology of Sanskrit Court Poetry,* translated by Daniel Ingalls, reprinted by permission of Harvard University Press.

"Riders" by Robert Frost; "For a Young Man Who Died" from *The Road to Downderry and Other Poems* by Margaret Widdemer, © 1932, © 1960 by Margaret Widdemer; and excerpt from *Anthony Adverse* by Hervey Allen; reprinted by permission of Holt, Rinehart and Winston, Inc.

"Rio Grande Pueblos" translated by Mary Austin from *American Rhythm;* "Little Girl, My String Bean" by Anne Sexton from *Live or Die;* "With Age, Wisdom" from *The Collected Poems of Archibald MacLeish;* and excerpt from *The Member of The Wedding* by Carson McCullers; and "Decade" from *The Complete Poetical Works of Amy Lowell,* © 1912; reprinted by permission of Houghton Mifflin Company.

"The Old Men," "Song to be Sung by the Father of Infant Female Children" and excerpt from "Let's Not Climb the Washington Monument Tonight" from *Verses from 1929 On* by Ogden Nash, © 1933; and excerpt from *Nobody Ever Died of Old Age* by Sharon R. Curtin; reprinted by permission of Little, Brown and Company.

Excerpt from the editorial "In Praise of Wrinkles" reprinted by permission of the *London Daily Mail,* London, England.

"The Garden," "The Long Hill," and "A Boy" by Sara Teasdale from *Collected Poems,*© 1920, renewed; "Winter" and "Wisdom" by Sara Teasdale from *Collected Poems,*© 1926, renewed; and "Mr. Flood's Party" by Edwin Arlington Robinson from *Collected Poems,*© 1921 by Edwin Arlington Robinson, renewed 1949 by Ruth Nivison; and excerpts from *Memoirs of Childhood and Youth* by Albert Schweitzer; reprinted by permission of Macmillan Publishing Co., Inc.

Excerpt from *Requiem For The Living* and "The Newborn" from *Pegasus and Other Poems* by C. Day Lewis, © C. Day Lewis, reprinted by permission of Harold Matson Co., Inc.

"Prayer for a Very New Angel" and "To an Older Woman" by Violet Alleyn Storey from *Green of The Year,* reprinted with permission of Meredith Coporation.

"Dirge Without Music" by Edna St. Vincent Millay and "Departure" by Edna St. Vincent Millay. *Collected Poems,* Harper & Row. Copyright © 1923, 1928, 1951, 1955 by Edna St. Vincent Millay and Norma Millay Ellis.

Excerpt from "Ortus" from *Personnae* by Ezra Pound, copyright © 1926 by Ezra Pound; and "Do Not Go Gentle into That Good Night" from *Collected Poems of Dylan Thomas;* reprinted by permission of New Directions Publishing Corp.

"What Is a Boy?" and "What Is a Girl?" by Allen Beck reprinted by permission of New England Mutual Life Insurance Company,© 1950.

Excerpt from *"Where Did You Go?" "Out." "What Did You Do?" "Nothing."* by Robert Paul Smith; and "Now Voyageur" from *Cloud, Stone, Sun, Vine, Poems, Selected and New,* © 1961 by May Sarton; reprinted by permission of W. W. Norton & Company, Inc.

Excerpts from "June in Limbo" by Marya Mannes, published in *Harper's* magazine, July, 1964,© 1964 by Marya Mannes, reprinted by permission of Harold Ober Associates Incorporated.

"Prayer Before Birth" from *The Collected Poems of Louis MacNeice,* edited by E. R. Dodds, copyright © The Estate of Louis MacNeice 1966. Reprinted by permission of Oxford University Press, Inc.

Excerpts from "Man Is the Meaning" and "A Thanksgiving for Children" by Kenneth L. Patton.

"Little" from *Everything and Anything* by Dorothy Aldis, © 1927 by Dorothy Aldis, reprinted by permission of G. P. Putnam's Sons.

Excerpt from *Gift From The Sea* by Anne Morrow Lindbergh; excerpts from *The New Years: A New Middle Age* by Anne Simon; excerpt from "To a Young Friend" from *The Green Leaf* by Robert Nathan; excerpt from "Innocence and Experience" from *God Speaks* by Charles Peguy; and excerpt from *The Journals of Andre Gide* by Andre Gide; reprinted by permission of Random House, inc., Alfred A. Knopf, Inc., and Pantheon Books.

Excerpt from Seneca, translated by Joyce Penny, from *Latin Lyrics,* reprinted by permission of Regency Press (London & New York) Ltd.

"Telos" by John Hall Wheelock from *Dear Men and Women,* © 1966 John Hall Wheelock, reprinted with the permission of Charles Scribner's Sons.

Excerpt from "Both Sides Now" by Joni Mitchell, © 1967 Siquomb Publishing Corp. All rights reserved. Reprinted by permission of Segel, Rubinstein & Gordon.

Excerpt from "Love and Marriage" by Ernest Havemann, *Life* magazine,© 1961, reprinted by permission of Time Inc.

"Coda" from *The Portable Dorothy Parker,*© 1928,© 1956 by Dorothy Parker; and "Little Old Lady in Lavender Silk" from *The Portable Dorothy Parker,* © 1931, © 1959 by Dorothy Parker; reprinted by permission of The Viking Press, Inc.

Excerpt from *The Transformations: Notes on Childhood* by Alastair Reid, © 1963 by Alastair Reid, reprinted with the permission of the author's agent, John Wolfers.

"The Unborn" by Julia Neely Finch from *Your Baby's Name,* reprinted by permission of The World Publishing Company.

Nancy Flowers/Bethel Agency

Contents

prologue

To everything there is a season, and a time for every purpose under heaven: A time to be born, and a time to die; a time to plant, and a time to pluck that which is planted . . . .

ECCLESIASTES III, 1-8

Over the long ages, man has been fascinated with his own life cycle, and sought to find meaning and purpose in the individual and collective human experience.

This anthology can be read merely for the sheer beauty of its words and photographs; it is a treasury of some of the world's outstanding thought and literature relating to the various stages in the life of man. But it also forms something of a traveler's guide for the journey upon which we are all embarked.

Where have we been, and where are we going? What can we expect to find beyond the next bend in the road? What is it like to be a child, or an old person? What insights have others gleaned along the way that may be of value in learning to live more fully at whatever age we have attained?

There is, of course, a difficulty in any arbitrary system of classification, particularly with so complex a subject as human life. The stages of life resist being forced into inflexible categories, bounded by a specific number of years. When does youth end, and the middle years begin? The answer is as individual as a fingerprint to each of us. We have all known people who were old at fifty, and others who were full of youthful vigor at ninety. Yet the fact remains that, if we live long enough, each of us will at some time during our lives pass through the successive stages chronicled herein.

Like the day that forms the structure of this collection, morning moves slowly into the brightness of midday, the shadows lengthen as the afternoon

wears on and dissolves into the darkness of evening. Precisely when each stage succeeds the last is not important, except as it alters the pace and substance of each individual life.

Because there is such an interrelationship between the various age groups, there were difficulties, too, in knowing where to place a number of the selections included. A mother writes about her alienation from her teenage daughter. Is this appropriate to the chapter on youth, or on the middle years? A woman no longer young writes about her childhood, and her hope that heaven will find her there again. Does this speak more clearly about what it is like to be a child, or to be old? A young man foresees the years ahead; an old man recalls his youth. In each of these cases, and many others, we were again forced to be arbitrary in our classifications, in order to give some form of literary structure to this vast, sprawling, unstructured thing called life.

The authors represented here speak about emotions, experiences, hopes and fears that have been echoed in our own lives, or may someday be. It is an eerie feeling to read a passage, thinking "How could he have known so precisely how I felt, but could never put into words?" — and then discover that its writer lived ten centuries ago, in a far-off land.

What is apparent throughout this book is the universality of human experience. Countless others throughout the ages have preceeded us upon this journey. Some were skilled enough to make notations along the way that have endured. What follows is a record of their travels, gathered together to help us see our own in fuller perspective.

All the world's a stage,
And all the men and women merely players.
They have their exits and their entrances;
And one man in his time plays many parts,
His act being seven ages. At first the infant,
Mewling and puking in the nurse's arms.
And then the whining school-boy, with his satchel
And shining morning face, creeping like snail
Unwillingly to school. And then the lover,
Sighing like a furnace, with a woeful ballad
Made to his mistress' eyebrow. Then a soldier,
Full of strange oaths, and bearded like the pard;
Jealous in honour, sudden and quick in quarrel,
Seeking the bubble reputation
Even in the cannon's mouth. And then the justice,

In fair round belly with good capon lined,
With eyes severe and beard of formal cut,
Full of wise saws and modern instances;
And so he plays his part. The sixth age shifts
Into the lean and slipper'd pantaloon,
With spectacles on nose and pouch on side;
His youthful hose, well saved, a world too wide
For his shrunk shank; and his big manly voice,
Turning again toward childish treble, pipes
And whistles in his sound. Last scene of all,
That ends this strange history,
Is second childishness, and mere oblivion,
Sans teeth, sans eyes, sans taste, sans everything.

from As You Like It, II
WILLIAM SHAKESPEARE

Forenoon and afternoon and night, —
    Forenoon,
And afternoon, and night, — Forenoon,
    and — what!
The empty song repeats itself. No
    more?
Yea, that is Life: make this forenoon
    sublime,
This afternoon a psalm, this night a
    prayer,
And Time is conquered, and thy crown
    is noon.

"Life"
EDWARD ROWLAND SILL

To each stage of existence has been allotted its appropriate quality, so that the weakness of childhood, the impetuosity of youth, the seriousness of middle age, the maturity of old age — each bears some of nature's fruit which must be garnered in its own season.

from "De Senectute"
CICERO

Time is the root of all this earth;
These creatures, who from Time
    had birth,
Within his bosom at the end
Shall sleep; Time hath nor enemy nor
    friend.

All we in one long caravan
Are journeying since the world
    began;
We know not whither, but we
    know
Time guideth at the front, and all must
    go.

Like as the wind upon the field
Bows every herb, and all must
    yield,
So we beneath Time's passing
    breath
Bow each in turn, — why tears for
birth or death?

"Time"
BHARTRIHARI (Sanskrit)

Clemens Kalischer

Life, like a dome of many colored glass, stains the white radiance of eternity.

PERCY BYSSHE SHELLEY

How small a portion of our life it is that we really enjoy! In youth we are looking forward to things that are to come; in old age we are looking backward to things that are gone past; in manhood, although we appear indeed to be more occupied in things that are present, yet even that is too often absorbed in vague determinations to be vastly happy on some future day when we have time.

CALEB C. COLTON

Life is a beautiful and winding lane, on either side bright flowers, beautiful butterflies, and tempting fruits, which we scarcely pause to admire and taste, so eager are we to hasten to an opening which we imagine will be more beautiful still. But by degrees, as we advance, the trees grow bleak, the flowers and butterflies fail, the fruits disappear, and we find we have arrived — to reach a desert waste.

GEORGE AUGUSTUS SALA

Max Tharpe

Hope writes the poetry of the boy, but memory that of the man. Man looks forward with smiles, but backward with sighs. Such is the wise providence of God. The cup of life is sweetest at the brim, the flavor is impaired as we drink deeper, and the dregs are made bitter that we may not struggle when it is taken from our lips.

ADOLPHE MONOD

Life does not count by years. Some suffer a lifetime in a day, and so grow old between the rising and setting of the sun.

AUGUSTA EVANS

I planted a ripe seed, and it split, and where it had been a green sprout appeared; but the seed disintegrated.

The green sprout grew, a thing of beauty, sent down roots, sent out leaves, budded, flowered, bore fruit, decayed and was itself a withered thing. I could not even keep the ripe seed.

Each in its time had its own peculiar beauty. All things change; nothing remains the same.

So, each in its time, each life in its every moment — the baby, the child, the youth, the lover, the parent, the aged — is at its ultimate state in each moment and passes on.

Pluck this moment as you would a precious flower; share it as if it were love, and let it go. Beauty and wonder lie all about you even now; they too, even as you, are never final, but always in process of being and becoming. Take, then, each moment as the perfect gift of life, knowing that you shall no more be able to hold it as it is than what is already past.

Even as you let go, another and yet different moment comes . . . .

ROBERT T. WESTON

14

Erika

dawn

The first pale rays of the morning sun break over the horizon, and the day begins. A child is born.

Man must stand in grave wonder at this moment. Whatever its circumstances, the creation of a new life is a fearsome and magnificent thing. In this tiny, squalling being lies all the vast potential inherent in humanity, to be shaped and formed in the days and the years ahead. That countless millions of babies have been born before in no way alters the splendor of this individual moment in time.

Among those who have written of infancy, there are myriad points of view. Much of what an author feels about the intrinsic character of life is reflected in the way he views this new creature.

To some, he is the embodiment of the innocence and beauty that life inevitably destroys; to others, a bright hope of the happier future that is attainable. Some are content simply to marvel at his incredible beauty and closeness to God, while others tremble at the enormity of what he must face in a frightening world.

Whatever the viewpoint, there is agreement that the advent of this tiny new life marks the beginning of an awesome adventure.

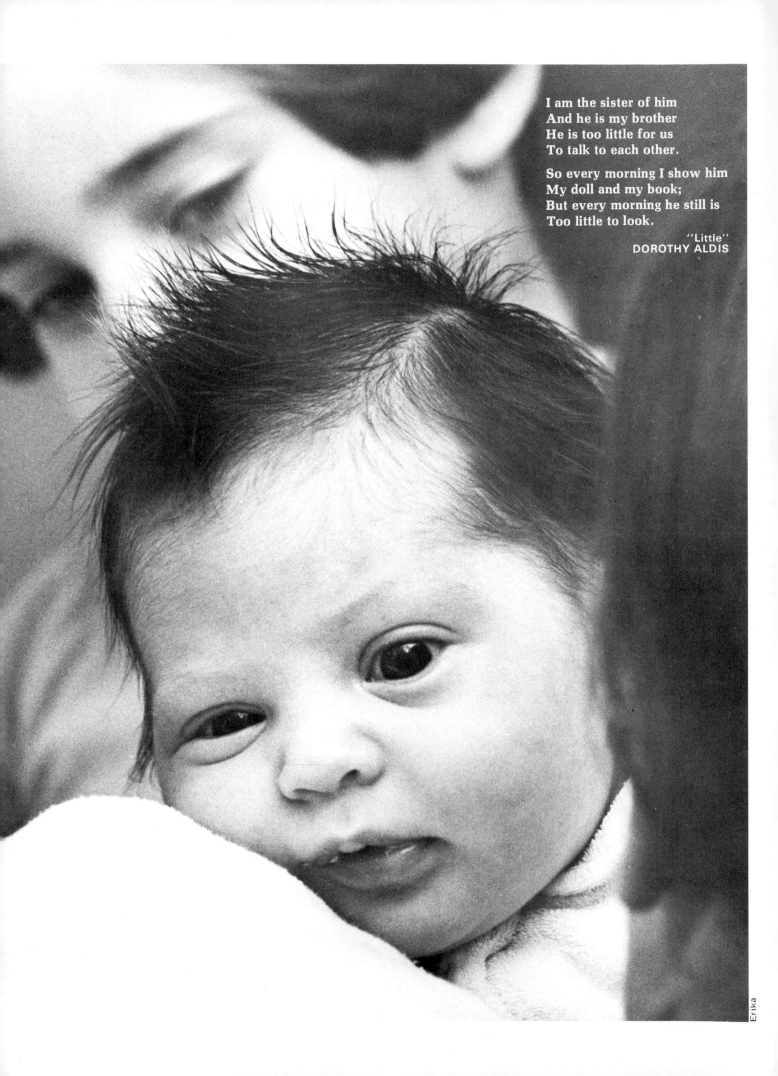

I am the sister of him
And he is my brother
He is too little for us
To talk to each other.

So every morning I show him
My doll and my book;
But every morning he still is
Too little to look.

"Little"
DOROTHY ALDIS

Erika

Thou art my very own,
A part of me,
Bone of my bone
And flesh of my flesh.
And thou shalt be
Heart of my heart
And brain of brain —
In years that are to come to me and
    thee . . . .
In a soft and silken chamber set
    apart —
Here, just beneath my happy
    heart, —
Thou didst lie at dreamy ease
While all my being paid
Its tribute unto thee.
What happy hours for thee and me!
As when a bird
Broods on its downy nest —
So would I sit
And watch the flit
Of idle shadows to and fro,
And brood upon my treasure hid
Within my willing flesh.
And when there stirred
A little limb — a tiny hand! —
What rapturous thrills of ecstasy
Shook all my being to its inmost
    citadel!
Ah! none but she who has borne
A child beneath her breast may know
What wondrous thrill and subtle spell
Comes from this wondrous woven
    band
That binds a mother to her unborn
    child
Within her womb.
As in the earth —
That fragrant tomb
Of all that lives, of man or beast —
Soft blossoms bud and bloom and
    swell,
So didst thou from my body gain
Sweet sustenance and royal feast.
Then through the gates of priceless
    pain
Thou camest to me — fair, so fair,
And so complete
From rose-tipped feet
To silken hair!
And there beneath each pearly lid,
There glowed a jewel — passing rare!

Erika

It moves and breathes! It slakes its
    thirst
At my all-abundant breast!
Oh moment born of life — of love!
Oh, rapture of all earth's high, high
    above!
Three lives in one —
By loving won!
My own — and thine —
Oh bond divine!
Our little child! Our little child!

"The Unborn"
JULIA NEELY FINCH

I am not yet born; O hear me.
Let not the bloodsucking bat or the rat or the stoat or the
    club-footed ghoul come near me.
I am not yet born, console me.
I fear that the human race may with tall walls wall me,
    with strong drugs dope me, with wise lies lure me,
        on black racks rack me, in blood-baths roll me.
I am not yet born; provide me
With water to dandle me, grass to grow for me, trees to talk
    to me, sky to sing to me, birds and a white light
        in the back of my mind to guide me.
I am not yet born; forgive me
For the sins that in me the world shall commit, my words
    when they speak me, my thoughts when they think me,
        my treason engendered by traitors beyond me,
            my life when they murder by means of my
                hands, my death when they live me.
I am not yet born; rehearse me
In the parts I must play and the cues I must take when
    old men lecture me, bureaucrats hector me, mountains
        frown at me, lovers laugh at me, the white
            waves call me to folly and the desert calls
                me to doom and the beggar refuses
                    my gift and my children curse me.
I am not yet born; O hear me,
Let not the man who is beast or who thinks he is God
    come near me.
I am not yet born; O fill me
With strength against those who would freeze my
    humanity, would dragoon me into a lethal automaton,
        would make me a cog in a machine, a thing with
            one face, a thing, and against all those
                who would dissipate my entirety, would
                    blow me like thistledown hither and
                        thither or hither and thither
                            like water held in the
                                hands would spill me.
Let them not make me a stone and let them not spill me.
Otherwise kill me.

"Prayer Before Birth"
LOUIS MacNEICE

20

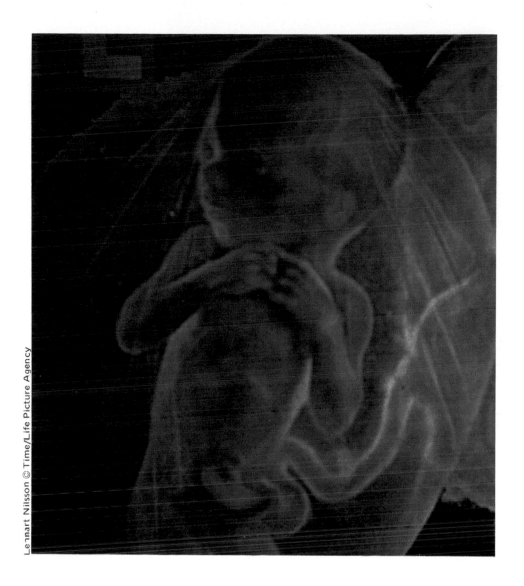

And so the children come.
And so they have been coming.
Always in the same way they come —
Born of the seed of man and woman.
No angels herald their beginnings,
No prophets predict their future courses,
No wise men see a star to point their way
To find the babe that may save mankind.

Yet each night a child is born is a holy night.
Fathers and Mothers —
Sitting beside their children's cribs —
Feel glory in the wond'rous sight of a life beginning.
They ask: ''When or how will this new life end?
Or will it ever end?''
Each night a child is born is a holy night.

from ''Each Night A Child Is Born''
SOPHIA LYON FAHS

Von Kenol/Katherine Young

This mannikin who just now
Broke prison and stepped free
Into his own identity —
Hand, foot and brow
A finished work, a breathing miniature —
Was still, one night ago
A hope, a dread, a mere shape we
Had lived with, only sure
Something would grow
Out of its coiled nine-months nonentity.

How like a blank sheet
His lineaments appear;
But there's invisible writing here
Which the day's heat
Will show: legends older than language, glum
Histories of the tribe,
Directives from his near and dear —
Charms, curses, rules of thumb —
He will transcribe
Into his own blood to write upon an heir.

Welcome to earth, my child!

We time-worn folk renew
Ourselves at your enchanted spring,
As though mankind's begun
Again in you.

from ''The Newborn''
C. DAY LEWIS

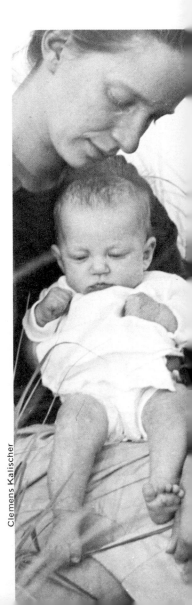

Clemens Kalischer

22

A baby's feet, like sea-shells pink,
Might tempt, should heaven see meet,
An angel's lips to kiss, we think,
A baby's feet.

Like rose-hued sea-flowers toward the heat
They stretch and spread and wink
Their ten soft buds that part and meet.

No flower-bells that expand and shrink
Gleam half so heavenly sweet,
As shine on life's untrodden brink
A baby's feet.

"A Baby's Feet"
ALGERNON SWINBURNE

Of all the joys that brighten suffering earth, what joy is welcomed like a
newborn child?

CAROLINE NORTON

Beautiful as is the morning of the day, so is the morning of life. — Fallen
though we are, there remains a purity, modesty, ingenuousness and
tenderness of conscience about childhood, that looks as if the glory of Eden
yet lingered over it, like the light of the day on the hilltops, at even, when
the sun is down.

THOMAS GUTHRIE

A babe in the house is a well-spring of pleasure, a messenger of peace and love, a resting place for innocence on earth, a link between angels and men.

MARTIN FARQUHAR TUPPER

A sweet new blossom of humanity, fresh fallen from God's own home, to flower on earth.

GERALD MASSEY

We are born into life — it is sweet, it is strange.
We lie still on the knee of a mild Mystery
Which smiles with a change;
But we doubt not of changes, we know not of spaces,
The Heavens seem as near as our mother's face is,
And we think we could touch all the stars that we see;
And the milk of our mother is white on our mouth;
And, with small, childish hands we are turning around
The apple of Life, which another has found.

from "A Rhapsody of Life's Progress"
ELIZABETH BARRETT BROWNING

Such a small beginning, newly growing —
So untouched by living, yet so knowing;
Miracle of hands and eyes and hair —
Thoughtfully aloof, yet so aware!
Love has wrought this marvel of creation;
Humble is our silent supplication.
Two who once the common roadway trod
Timidly stand hand in hand with God.

"Such a Little Child"
DOROTHY ASHBY POWNAL

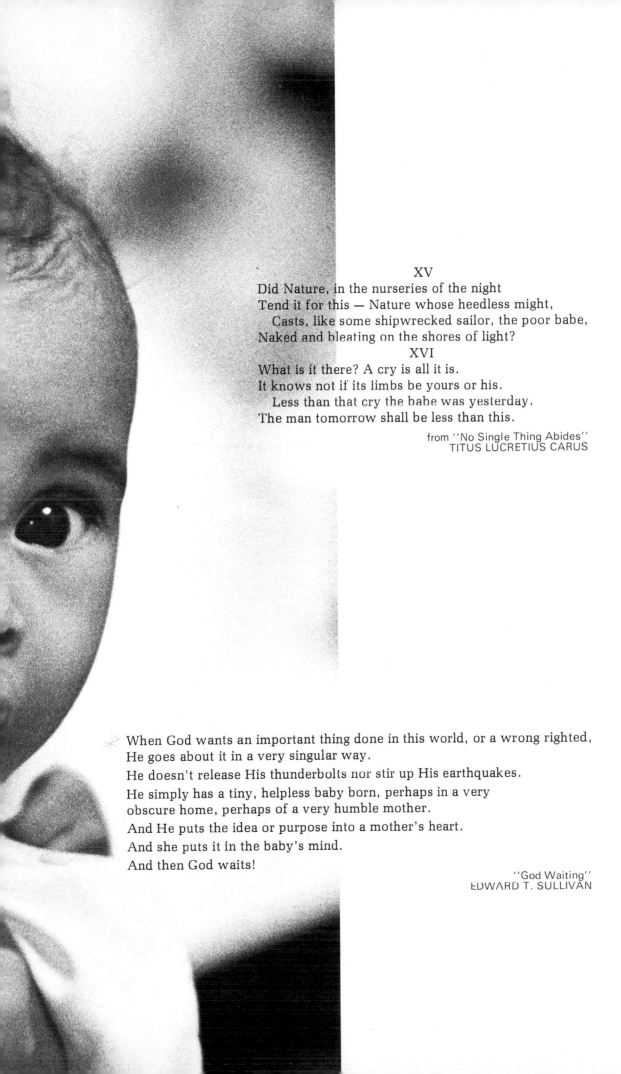

XV

Did Nature, in the nurseries of the night
Tend it for this — Nature whose heedless might,
  Casts, like some shipwrecked sailor, the poor babe,
Naked and bleating on the shores of light?

XVI

What is it there? A cry is all it is.
It knows not if its limbs be yours or his.
  Less than that cry the babe was yesterday.
The man tomorrow shall be less than this.

from ''No Single Thing Abides''
TITUS LUCRETIUS CARUS

When God wants an important thing done in this world, or a wrong righted,
He goes about it in a very singular way.

He doesn't release His thunderbolts nor stir up His earthquakes.

He simply has a tiny, helpless baby born, perhaps in a very
obscure home, perhaps of a very humble mother.

And He puts the idea or purpose into a mother's heart.

And she puts it in the baby's mind.

And then God waits!

''God Waiting''
EDWARD T. SULLIVAN

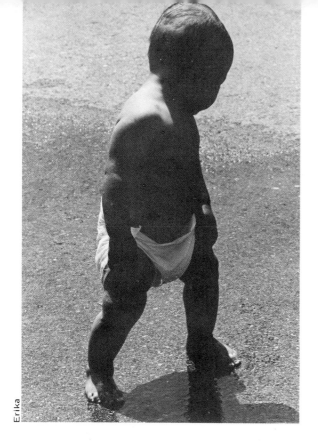

Erika

De Wys, Inc.

O child of man,
Wombed in dark waters you retell
Millenniums, image the terrestrial span
From an unwitting cell
To the new soul within her intricate shell.
O child of man.

O child of man
Whose infant eyes and groping mind
Meet chaos and create the world again,
You for yourself must find
The toils we know, the truths we have divined
Yes, child of man.

from ''Requiem for the Living''
C. DAY LEWIS

Clemens Kalischer

28

Sweet and low, sweet and low,
Wind of the western sea,
Low, low, breathe and blow,
Wind of the western sea!
Over the rolling waters go,
Come from the dying moon, and blow,
Blow him again to me;
While my little one, while my pretty one sleeps.

Sleep and rest, sleep and rest,
Father will come to thee soon;
Rest, rest, on mother's breast,
Father will come to thee soon;
Father will come to his babe in the nest,
Silver sails all out of the west
Under the silver moon;
Sleep, my little one, sleep, my pretty one, sleep.

"Sweet and Low"
ALFRED LORD TENNYSON

Clemens Kalischer

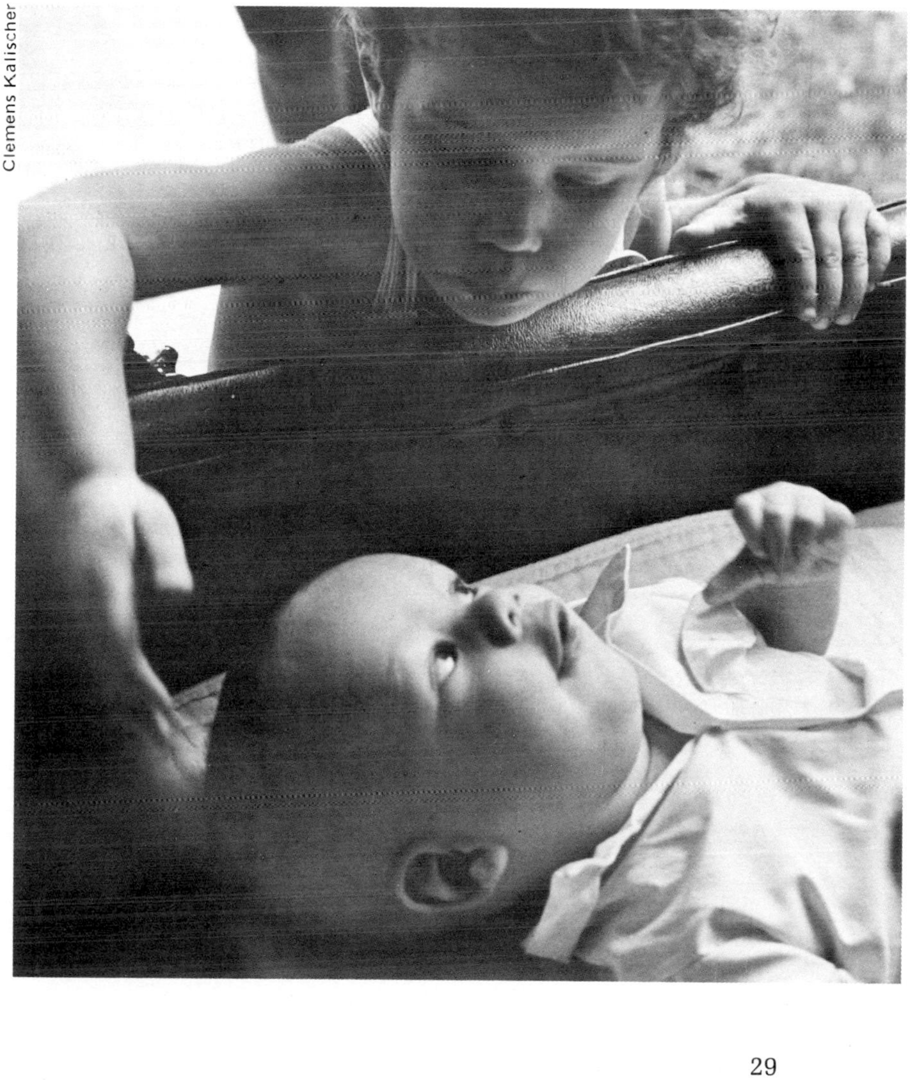

Man, a dunce uncouth,
Errs in age and youth:
Babies know the truth.
ALGERNON SWINBURNE

Every child born into
the world is a new
thought of God, an
ever-fresh and
radiant possibility.
KATE DOUGLAS WIGGIN

29

Behold the child, the visitor. He has come from nowhere, for he was not before this, and it is nowhere that he goes, wherefore he is called a visitor, for the visitor is one who comes from the unknown to stay but awhile and then to the unknown passes on again.

The child has come forth out of the great womb of the earth. The child has come forth to stand with star dust in his hair, with the rush of planets in his blood, his heart beating out the seasons of eternity, with a shining in his eyes like the sunlight, with hands to shape with that same force that shaped him out of the raw stuff of the universe.

When one baby is born it is the symbol of all birth and life, and therefore all men must rejoice and smile, and all men must lose their hearts to a child.

from Man Is the Meaning
KENNETH L. PATTON

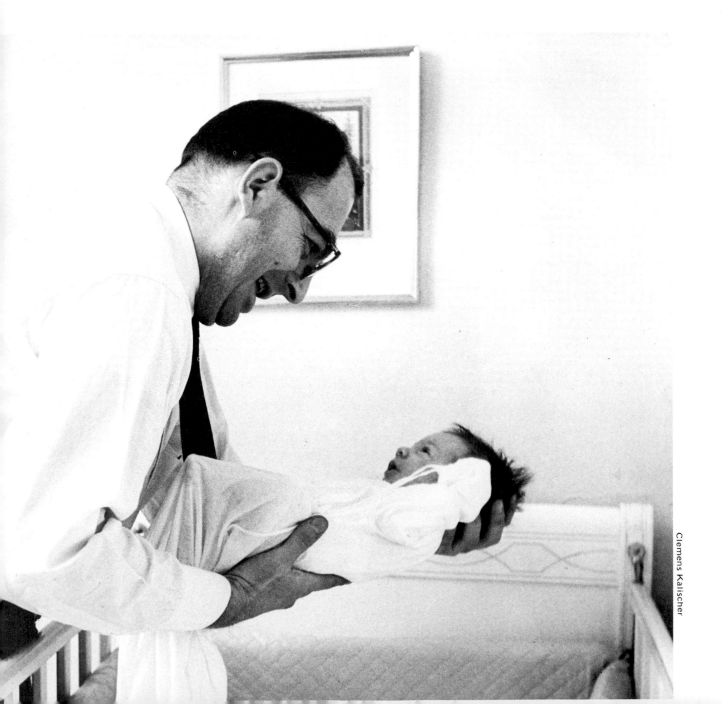

Clemens Kalischer

Erika

Erika

Erika

34

from spiralling ecstatically this

proud nowhere of earth's most prodigious night
blossoms a newborn babe: around him, eyes
— gifted with every keener appetite
than mere unmiracle can quite appease —
humbly in their imagined bodies kneel
(over time space doom dream while floats the whole

perhapsless mystery of paradise)

mind without soul may blast some universe
to might have been, and stop ten thousand stars
but not one heartbeat of this child; nor shall
even prevail a million questionings
against the silence of his mother's smile

— whose only secret all creation sings

"from spiralling ecstatically this"
E.E. CUMMINGS

Erika

Our birth is but a sleep and a forgetting:
The Soul that rises with us, our life's Star,
  Hath had elsewhere its setting,
  And cometh from afar:
  Not in entire forgetfulness,
And not in utter nakedness,
But trailing clouds of glory do we come
  From God who is our home.
WILLIAM WORDSWORTH

Heaven lies around us in our infancy.
from "Intimations of Immortality"
WILLIAM WORDSWORTH

Out of the mouths of babes and sucklings thou hast perfected praise.
MATTHEW XXI, 16

Some, admiring what motives to mirth infants meet with in their silent and solitary smiles, have resolved . . . that then they converse with angels.
from A Pisgah-Sight of Palestine
THOMAS FULLER

O Hesperus, thou bringest all good things —
  Home to the weary, to the hungry cheer,
To the young bird the parent's brooding wings,
  The welcome stall to the o'erlabored steer;
Whate'er of peace about our hearthstone clings,
  Whate'er our household gods protect of dear,
Are gathered round us by thy look of rest;
Thou bringst the child too to its mother's breast.
"Hesperus the Bringer"
SAPPHO

Who would not tremble and rather choose to die than to be a baby again, if he were given such a choice?

from The City of God, XVII
ST. AUGUSTINE

Here we have a baby. It is composed of a bald head and a pair of lungs.

from The Tribune Primer
EUGENE FIELD

From the dark womb, like an uncleanliness,
On a heap of gathered foulness I was cast,
Unwashed from filth, with rags for swaddling-clothes,
My mother stretched to me a withered breast
And stilled me with the bitter milk of madness.
And in my heart a viper made its nest
And sucks my blood to render it in poison.
Where can I hide me from its burning fangs?
God! answer me with either life or death.

from "Night"
CHAIM NACHMAN BIALIK

How have I labored?
How have I not labored
To bring her soul to birth,
To give these elements a name and a centre!
She is beautiful as the sunlight, and as fluid.
She has no name, and no place.
How have I labored to bring her soul into separation
To give her a name and her being.

"Ortus"
EZRA POUND

The babe
In the dim newness of its being feels
The impulses of sublunary things.

from Queen Mab, VI
PERCY BYSSHE SHELLEY

Newborn, on the naked sand
Nakedly lay it.
Next to the earth mother,
That it may know her;
Having good thoughts of her, the food giver.

Newborn, we tenderly
In our arms take it,
Making good thoughts.
House-god, be entreated,
That it may grow from childhood to manhood,
Happy, contented;
Beautifully walking
The trail to old age.
Having good thoughts of the earth its mother,
That she may give it the fruits of her being.
Newborn, on the naked sand
Nakedly lay it.

RIO GRANDE PUEBLOS
(tr. Mary Austin)

He is so small, he does not know
The summer sun, the winter snow;
The spring that ebbs and comes again,
All this is far beyond his ken.

A little world he feels and sees;
His mother's arms, his mother's knees;
He hides his face against her breast,
And does not care to learn the rest.

"Six Weeks Old"
CHRISTOPHER MORLEY

Erika

morning

Everything is new in the morning of life.

The child explores a new land, learns a new language, discovers in a thousand different ways both its joys and its fears.

Because he is an explorer, he experiences each new thing with all his senses open. Show him a dandelion, a puppy, a snowfall; he will feel, taste, smell, listen, examine. He will wonder, and question. He will play with words, and with ideas.

If he is very lucky, he is loved and cared for; and that knowledge gives him a secure base from which to launch his explorations, and a safe harbor in which to rest. It will give him courage to venture beyond the familiar into uncharted territory, not afraid to be a little frightened.

By the same token, no one is as pitifully vulnerable as a child in an unloving environment.

Most adults remember childhood (if theirs was secure and happy) as a halcyon time when an all-powerful mommy and daddy would take care of all problems and make all decisions. We forget the frustrations inherent in such a situation for the child who is at the mercy of his parents' omnipotence, who must always do what others think is best for him, or suffer the consequences.

What is it like to be a child, or to love a child? Authors over the years have sought to recreate that world in words, and photographers find one of their richest fields in the study of children.

in Just-
spring   when the world is mud-
luscious the little
lame balloonman

whistles   far   and wee

and eddieanbill come
running from marbles and
piracies and it's
spring

when the world is puddle-wonderful

the queer
old balloonman whistles
far   and   wee
and bettyandisbel come dancing

from hop-scotch and jump-rope and

it's
spring
and
     the
          goat-footed

balloonMan   whistles
far
and
wee

"chanson innocent"
E.E. CUMMINGS

Now this is the day.
Our child,
Into the daylight
You will go out standing.
Preparing for your day.

Our child, it is your day,
This day.

May your road be fulfilled.
In your thoughts may we live,
May we be the ones
   whom your thoughts will embrace,
May you help us all to finish our roads.

ZUNI INDIANS

45

I devise to children the banks of the brooks and the golden sands beneath the waters thereof, and the odors of the willows that dip therein, and the white clouds that float high over the giant trees. And I leave to them the long days to be merry in, in a thousand ways, and the night and the moon, and the train of the Milky Way to wonder at.

from Last Will And Testament
CHARLES LOUNSBURY

The hearts of small children are delicate organs. A cruel beginning in this world can twist them into curious shapes. The heart of a child can shrink so that forever afterward it is hard and pitted as the seed of a peach. Or again, the heart of such a child may fester and swell until it is a misery to carry within the body, easily chafed and hurt by the most ordinary things.

from The Member Of The Wedding
CARSON McCULLERS

46

Four is too big for his breeches,
Knows infinitely more than his mother,
Four is a matinee idol
To Two-and-a-Half, his brother.
Four is a lyric composer,
Ranconteur extraordinaire,
Four gets away with murder,
Out of line, and into hair.
Where Four is, there dirt is also,
And nails and lengths of twine,
Four is Mr. Fix-it
And all of his tools are mine.
Four barges into everything
(Hearts, too) without a knock.
Four will be five on the twelfth of July,
And I wish I could stop the clock.

"Four"
ELISE GIBBS

Douglas Green

A boy has two jobs. One is just being a boy. The other is growing up to be a man.

from "Address to the Fiftieth Anniversary
Celebration of the Boys' Clubs of America,"
May 21, 1956
HERBERT HOOVER

A boy is a magical creature — you can lock him out of your workshop, but you can't lock him out of your heart. You can get him out of your study, but you can't get him out of your mind. Might as well give up — he is your captor, your jailor, your boss, and your master — a freckled-faced, pint-sized, cat-chasing bundle of noise. But when you come home at night with only the shattered pieces of your hopes and dreams he can mend them like new with two magic words — "Hi Dad!"

from "What Is a Boy?"
ALAN BECK

Of all people children are the most imaginative. They abandon themselves without reserve to every illusion. No man, whatever his sensibility may be, is ever affected by Hamlet or Lear as a little girl is affected by the story of poor Red Riding-hood.

from Milton
J.B. MACAULAY

Gene Ahrens

Beautiful!

Rowland Scherman/Bethel Agency

Children are entitled to their otherness, as anyone is; and when we reach them, as we sometimes do, it is generally on a point of sheer delight, to us so astonishing, but to them so natural.

from Places, Poems, Preoccupations
ALASTAIR REID

. . . Wherever they go, and whatever happens to them on the way, in that enchanted place on the top of the Forest, a little boy and his Bear will always be playing.

closing lines in the last
of the Winnie-the-Pooh series; recalled in
reports of his death, Jan. 31, 1956
A.A. MILNE

50

God bless all little boys who look like Puck
With wide eyes, wider mouths and stickup ears,
Rash little boys who stay alive by luck
And heaven's favor in this world of tears.

ARTHUR GUITERMAN

I remember, I remember
The fir-trees dark and high;
I used to think their slender tops
Were close against the sky:
It was a childish ignorance
But now 'tis little joy
To know I'm farther off from heav'n
Than when I was a boy.

THOMAS HOOD

Katherine Young

Call not that man wretched, who, whatever else he suffers as to pain inflicted or pleasure denied, has a child for whom he hopes and on whom he dotes.

SAMUEL TAYLOR COLERIDGE

Children are God's apostles, day by day sent forth to preach of love and hope and peace.

JAMES RUSSELL LOWELL

Train up a child in the way he should go; and when he is old, he will not depart from it.

PROVERBS XXII, 6

Suffer little children to come unto me, and forbid them not; for of such is the kingdom of God.

MARK X, 14

Pretty much all the honest truth-telling there is in the world is done by children.

OLIVER WENDELL HOLMES

Except ye be converted, and become as little children, ye shall not enter into the kingdom of heaven.

MATTHEW XVIII, 3

Max Tharpe

Max Tharpe

Little girls are the nicest things that happen to people. They are born with a little bit of angel-shine about them and though it wears thin sometimes, there is always enough left to lasso your heart — even when they are sitting in the mud, or crying temperamental tears, or parading up the street in mother's best clothes.

A little girl can be sweeter (and badder) oftener than anyone else in the world. She can jitter around, and stomp, and make funny noises that frazzle your nerves, yet just when you open your mouth, she stands there demure with that special look in her eyes. A girl is innocence playing in the mud, Beauty standing on its head, and Motherhood dragging a doll by the foot.

Girls are available in five colors — black, white, red, yellow, or brown, yet Mother Nature always manages to select your favorite color when you place your order. They disprove the law of supply and demand — there are millions of little girls, but each is as precious as rubies.

God borrows from many creatures to make a little girl. He uses the song of a bird, the squeal of a pig, the stubbornness of a mule, the antics of a monkey, the spryness of a grasshopper, the curiosity of a cat, the speed of a gazelle, the slyness of a fox, the softness of a kitten, and to top it all off He adds the mysterious mind of a woman.

A little girl likes new shoes, party dresses, small animals, first grade, noise makers, the girl next door, dolls, make-believe, dancing lessons, ice cream, kitchens, coloring books, make-up, cans of water, going visiting, tea parties, and one boy. She doesn't care so much for visitors, boys in general, large dogs, hand-me-downs, straight chairs, vegetables, snow suits, or staying in the front yard. She is loudest when you are thinking, the prettiest when she has provoked you, the busiest at bedtime, the quietest when you want to show her off, and the most flirtatious when she absolutely must not get the best of you again.

Who else can cause you more grief, joy, irritation, satisfaction, embarrasment, and genuine delight than this combination of Eve, Salome, and Florence Nightingale? She can muss up your home, your hair, and your dignity — spend your money, your time, and your temper — then just when your patience is ready to crack, her sunshine peeks through and you've lost again.

Yes, she is a nerve-racking nuisance, just a noisy bundle of mischief. But when your dreams tumble down and the world is a mess — when it seems you are pretty much of a fool after all — she can make you a king when she climbs on your knee and whispers, ''I love you best of all!''

''What Is a Girl?''
ALAN BECK

God, God, be lenient her first night there!
   The crib she slept in was so near my bed.
Her blue and white wool blanket was so soft
   The pillow hollowed so, to fit her head.

Teach me that she'll not want small rooms or me
When she has you and Heaven's immensity!

I always left a light out in the hall.
   I hoped to make her fearless in the dark.
And yet, she was so small, one little light,
   Not in the room, — it scarcely mattered. — Hark!!

No! No! She seldom cried. — God, not too far
For her to see, this first night, light a star!

And in the morning, when she first wakes up,
   I always kissed her on the left cheek where
The dimple was, and oh, I wet the brush —
   It made it easier to curl her hair!

Just, just tomorrow morning, God, I pray,
When she wakes up, do things for her my way!

               "A Prayer for a Very New Angel"
               VIOLET ALLEYN STORY

Von Kenol/Katherine Young

Thou happy, happy elf!
(But stop — first let me kiss away that tear) —
  Thou tiny image of myself!
(My love, he's poking peas into his ear!)
    Thou merry, laughing sprite!
    With spirits feather-light,
Untouched by sorrow, and unsoiled by sin —
(Good Heavens! the child is swallowing a pin!)

    Thou little tricksy Puck!
With antics toy so funnily bestuck,
Light as the singing bird that wings the air —
(The door! The door! He'll tumble down the stair!)
    Thou darling of thy sire!
(Why, Jane, he'll set his pinafore afire!)
    Thou imp of mirth and joy!
In love's dear chain so strong and bright a link
Thou idol of thy parents — (Drat the boy! There goes my ink!)

    Thou cherub — but of earth;
Fit playfellow for fays, by moonlight pale,
  In harmless sport and mirth —
(That dog will bite him if he pulls its tail!)
    Thou human humming-bee, extracting honey
From every blossom in the world that blows,
    Singing in youth's elysium ever sunny —
(Another tumble! — that's his precious nose!)

    Thy father's pride and hope!
(He'll break the mirror with that skipping-rope!)
With pure heart newly stamped from Nature's mint —
(Where did he learn that squint?)
    Thou young domestic dove!
(He'll have that jug off, with another shove!)
    Dear nursling of the Hymeneal nest!
    (Are those torn clothes his best?)
    Little epitome of man!
(He'll climb upon the table, that's his plan!)
Touched with the beauteous tints of dawning life —
    (He's got a knife!)

    Thou enviable being!
No storms, no clouds, in thy blue sky foreseeing,
    Play on, play on,
    My elfin John!
Toss the light ball — bestride the stick —
(I knew so many cakes would make him sick!)
With fancies, buoyant as the thistle-down,
Prompting the face grotesque, and antic brisk,
    With many a lamb-like frisk —
(He's got the scissors, snipping at your gown!)

    Thou pretty opening rose!
(Go to your mother, child, and wipe your nose!)
Balmy and breathing music like the south —

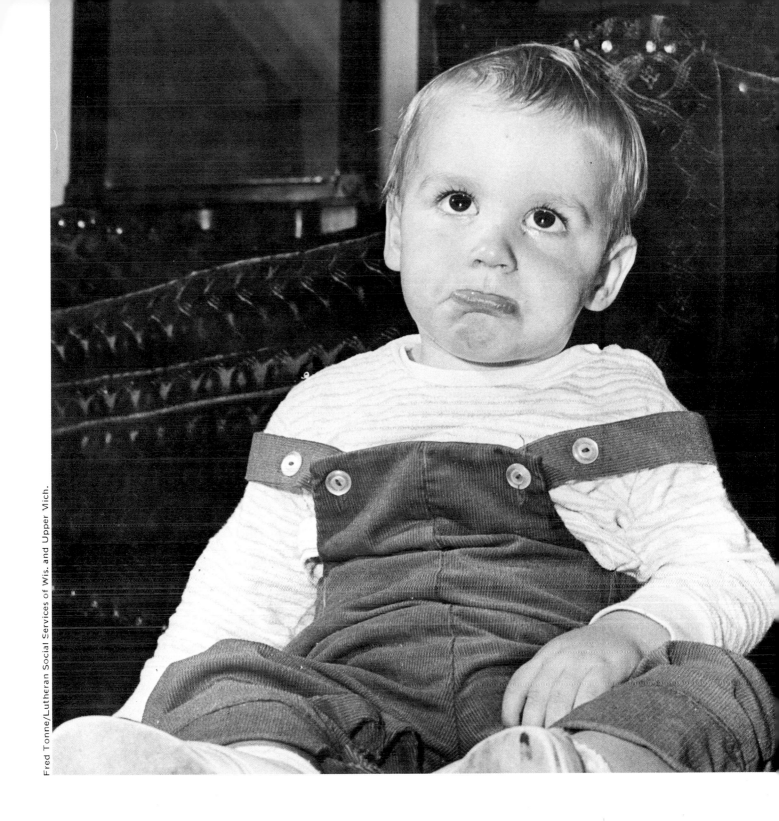

(He really brings my heart into my mouth!)
Fresh as the morn, and brilliant as its star —
(I wish that window had an iron bar!)
Bold as a hawk, yet gentle as the dove —
  (I'll tell you what, my love,
I cannot write, unless he's sent above!)

"Ode to My Little Son"
THOMAS HOOD

Douglas Green

The children of Berlin are heavenly-sweet;
Like gay, earth-bound angels they sing in the street.

And these innocent small ones are held the more dear
Because of our yesterdays, darkened with fear.

For we mothers remember the death that once fell
Through pale nights of horror; through red nights of hell.

And still as we pray they'll know years bright and free,
A Wall casts its shade where tomorrow should be.

"The Children of Berlin"
ETHEL BOEHM FOTH

Max Tharpe

57

Max Tharpe

How do you like to go up in a swing,
  Up in the air so blue?
Oh, I do think it the pleasantest thing
  Ever a child can do!

Up in the air and over the wall,
  Till I can see so wide,
Rivers and trees and cattle and all
  Over the countryside —

Till I look down on the garden green,
  Down on the roof so brown —
Up in the air I go flying again,
  Up in the air and down!

''The Swing''
ROBERT LOUIS STEVENSON

Honey, there will be a hoop
And hills to roll it down . . .
(God couldn't give a little boy
The burden of a crown.)

He'll show you lots of trees to climb
And where he keeps the swings.
(God, let him have a ball and bat
Instead of shining wings!)

And will He let you sail a kite
Up where the sky is clear,
Without tall buildings stooping down?
Of course He will, my dear!

Now close your eyes . . . I'll kiss them shut
The way I always do.
(I must — I must not cry, dear God,
Until he's safe with you!)

"Farewell to a Little Boy"
HELEN WELSHIMER

My child, we were two children,
Small, merry by childhood's law;
We used to creep to the henhouse,
And hide ourselves in the straw.

We crowed like cocks, and whenever
The passers near us drew —
"Cock-a-doodle!" they thought
'Twas a real cock that crew.

The boxes about our courtyard
We carpeted to our mind,
And lived there both together —
Kept house in a noble kind.

The neighbor's old cat often
Came to pay us a visit;
(We have made the very same speeches
Each with a compliment in it.)

Larry Fried

After her health we asked,
Our care and regard to evince;
(We have made the very same speeches
To many an old cat since.)

We also sat and wisely
Discoursed, as old folks do,
Complaining how all went better
In those good old times we knew; —

How love, and truth, and believing
Had left the world to itself,
And how so dear was the coffee,
And how so rare was the pelf.

The children's games are over,
The rest is over with youth —
The world, the good games, the good times,
The belief, and the love, and the truth.

from "Mein Kind, Wir Waren Kinder"
HEINRICH HEINE

Berne Greene

I love these little people; and it is not a slight thing, when they, who are so fresh from God, love us.

CHARLES DICKENS

Call not that man wretched, who, whatever ills he suffers, has a child to love.

ROBERT SOUTHEY

Childhood has no forebodings; but then it is soothed by no memories of outlived sorrow.

GEORGE ELIOT

The child's grief throbs against its little heart as heavily as the man's sorrow; and the one finds as much delight in his kite or drum, as the other in striking the springs of enterprise, or soaring on the wings of fame.

EDWIN HUBBELL CHAPIN

All the gestures of children are graceful; the reign of distortion and unnatural attitudes commences with the introduction of the dancing master.

SIR JOSHUA REYNOLDS

The smallest children are nearest to God, as the smallest planets are nearest to the sun.

JEAN PAUL RICHTER

The plays of natural lively children are the infancy of art. — Children live in a world of imagination and feeling. — They invest the most insignificant object with any form they please, and see in it whatever they wish to see.

ADAM OEHLENSCHLAGER

Where children are, there is the golden age.

NOVALIS

Children sweeten labors, but they make misfortunes more bitter. — They increase the cares of life, but they mitigate the remembrance of death.

from Essays, VII
FRANCIS BACON

Childhood and genius have the same master-organ in common — inquisitiveness. — Let childhood have its way, and as it began where genius begins, it may find what genius finds.

EDWARD GEORGE BULWER-LYTTON

Children have neither a past nor a future; therefore they enjoy the present — which seldom happens to us.

JEAN DE LA BRUYERE

Algimantas Kezys, S.J.

Lying awake at night, knuckling my eyeballs so that I could see the flashes of light, the fireworks that only I knew about. Taking off the rubber band that I had wrapped around my thumb, tight, so that I could feel the prickles, the electricity, the exquisite torture of the slow removal of the garter. Going to sleep with my right big toe in my left hand, my right arm wrapped around my head holding the lobe of my left ear, to find out if I would wake up that way in the morning. Sitting on the back steps with my friend and a milk bottle, putting in a piece of licorice, and some medicine he had found when his mother cleaned out the medicine chest, and some salt and some pepper and a bit of chocolate, some raspberry jam and a piece of iron, a little ketchup and a rubber band, water and milk and a little square of watercolor paint prized out of my sister's paintbox. Shaking it up and wishing we had something to make it fizz, and daring each other to drink it, and tasting it, and saying it's good, it really is *good*.

You see, it never occurred to us that there was anything wrong in doing nothing, so long as we kept out of the way of grownups. These days, you see a kid lying on his back and looking blank and you begin to wonder what's wrong with him. There's nothing wrong with him, except he's thinking. He's trying to find out whether he breathes differently when he's thinking about it than when he's just breathing. He's seeing how long he can sit there without blinking. He is considering whether his father is meaner than Carl's father, he is wondering who he would be if his father hadn't married his mother, whether there is somewhere in the world somebody who is exactly like him in every detail up to and including the fact that the other one is sitting there thinking whether there is someone who is exactly like him in every detail. He is trying to arrive at some conclusion about his thumb.

But when we were kids, we had the sense to keep these things to ourselves. We didn't go around asking grownups about them. They obviously didn't know. We asked other kids. They knew. I think we were right about grownups being the natural enemies of kids, because we knew that what they wanted us to do was to be like them. And that was for the birds.

from "Where Did You Go?" "Out."
"What Did You Do?" "Nothing."
ROBERT PAUL SMITH

Some day I shall go to Heaven and be with my own people.
I shall be a little girl then, silent, with long brown ringlets
And staid old-fashioned ways, and wondering eyes that are quiet.
In heaven is an old house, a house that I knew aforetime,
(Not the house that I passed last week, so dingy and shrunken
With the willows cut away and so little a porch and garden,
Not that pitiful place. *My* house is safe in Heaven.)

I shall go up the walk — a long way for little footsteps —
And climb the steps, that are high, steps scarcely made for children;
Passing the vines on the porch and pulling a leaf as I pass them
From the branch that I always reached to, nearly stripped by my fingers.

They will be waiting for me in the old stiff room by the lamplight,
And I shall be quiet a little — so happy, because of returning
Back to the shelter of Heaven; to the dark carved wood of the sofa
I had thought burned long ago; and the Parian vase, not broken,
And the faces I never can find found now, and smiling a welcome
Down on my speechless face. Their arms will go out to hold me,
And they will say, "What is it? What troubles you, little dear one?"

And I will press more close against the kind arms around me,
And tell them, "Only a dream, a dream I have almost forgotten,
Of being in many strange places, and never finding you, never;
Of things I did that were hard, and people who were not patient,
Of being tired, and strange people who praised me or mocked me or hated,
And I was too old for lilacs or hollowing willow-whistles,
Or hearing voices say gently, "Ah, well, she is only a child . . ."
A hard and a dreary dream!

                      And the arms will hold me closer,
And I shall feel the kind eyes smile over my head through their glasses,
To the other eyes that love me, half pride, half loving amusement;
"She was always a strange little child, with strange little thoughts, our dear
    one:
It was only a dream, my darling, and dreams are nothing, mean nothing;
You must play in the air tomorrow, and gather us bunches of flowers;
The grapes are purple now; you shall come and help us cut them,
When you went they were only blossoms. You have been too long from
    Heaven:
You are tired with traveling here. You must sleep now, and sleep without
    dreaming."

So I shall lie in my bed with the soft low light beyond me
And the wrinkled hand over mine with the thin gold ring on its finger,
Hearing her murmured stories of long ago in the farmlands
When she was little as I. Till the lids fall over my eyes,
And I am asleep in peace, knowing surely that I shall awaken
In Heaven, always in Heaven! where love is forever and ever . . . .
Some day I shall go to Heaven and be with my own people.

"Road's End"
MARGARET WIDDEMER

Abbas-Sipa/Liaison Agency

Max Tharpe

How can I say that I've known
just what you know and just where you are?

What I want to say is, let your body in,
let it tie you in,
in comfort.
What I want to say,
is that there is nothing in your body that lies.
All that is new is telling the truth.

I'm here, that somebody else,
an old tree in the background.
You, stand still at your door,
sure of yourself, a white stone, a good stone —
as exceptional as laughter
you will strike fire,
that new thing!

from ''Little Girl, My String Bean''
ANNE SEXTON

The childhood shows the man
As morning shows the day.

from Paradise Regained, IV
JOHN MILTON

Childhood knows the human heart.

from Tamerlane, VII
EDGAR ALLAN POE

The young child is looking in the world to find himself — reflected in a mirror with a thousand faces.

MARIA MONTESSORI

✱Children are the world's most valuable resource and its best hope for the future.

JOHN F. KENNEDY

The great men and the doctors understand not the word of God, but it is revealed to the humble and to children.

from Table-Talk, XIV
MARTIN LUTHER

No man can tell but he that loves his children how many delicious accents makes a man's heart dance in the pretty conversation of those dear pledges; their childishness, their stammering, their little angers, their innocence, their imperfections, their necessities, are so many little emanations of joy and comfort to him that delights in their persons and society.

from Twenty-seven Sermons, XVII
JEREMY TAYLOR

✱ If you wish to study men you must not neglect to mix with the society of children.

from The Moral Instructor
JESSE TORREY

When I consider how little of a rarity children are, — that every street and blind alley swarms with them, — that the poorest people commonly have them in most abundance, — how often they turn out ill, and defeat the fond hopes of their parents, taking to vicious courses, which end in poverty, disgrace, the gallows, &c. — I cannot for my life tell what cause for pride there can possibly be in having them.

from A Bachelor's Complaint of the
Behavior of Married People
CHARLES LAMB

You can do anything with children if you only play with them.
BISMARCK

Do ye hear the children weeping, O my brothers?
from ''The Cry of the Children''
ELIZABETH BARRETT BROWNING

Lilo Raymond/Bethel Agency

Life has loveliness to sell,
  All beautiful and splendid things,
Blue waves whitened on a cliff,
  Soaring fire that sways and sings,
And children's faces looking up
Holding wonder like a cup.

from "Barter"
SARA TEASDALE

Children think not of what is past, nor what is to come, but enjoy the present time, which few of us do.

JEAN DE LA BRUYERE

Babies do not want to hear about babies; they like to be told of giants and castles, and of somewhat which can stretch and stimulate their little minds.

SAMUEL JOHNSON

I believe the power of observation in numbers of very young children to be quite wonderful for its closeness and accuracy. Indeed, I think that most grown men who are remarkable in this respect, may with greater propriety be said not to have lost the faculty, than to have acquired it; the rather, as I generally observe such men to retain a certain freshness, and gentleness, and capacity of being pleased, which are also an inheritance they have preserved from their childhood.

CHARLES DICKENS

I would rather see one of my children's faces kindle at the sight of the quay at Calais than be offered the chance of exploring by myself the palaces of Peking.

J. B. PRIESTLEY

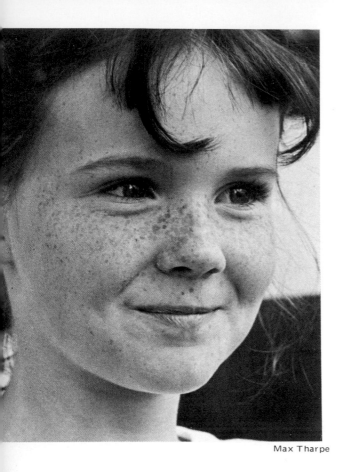

Max Tharpe

Behold the Child among his new-born blisses,
A six years' Darling of a pigmy size!
See, where 'mid work of his own hand he lies,
Fretted by sallies of his mother's kisses,
With light upon him from his father's eyes!
See, at his feet, some little plan or chart,
Some fragment from his dream of human life,
Shaped by himself with newly-learned art;
    A wedding or a festival,
    A mourning or a funeral;
      And this hath now his heart,
    And unto this he frames his song:
      Then will he fit his tongue
To dialogues of business, love, or strife;
    But it will not be long
    Ere this be thrown aside,
    And with new joy and pride
The little Actor cons another part;
Filling from time to time his "humorous stage"
With all the Persons, down to palsied Age,
That Life brings with her in her equipage;
    As if his whole vocation
    Were endless imitation.

from "Intimations of Immortality"
WILLIAM WORDSWORTH

Unto us our children are given as an encouragement of hope and strength.
What matter if our bodies stiffen and age, if our hearts falter and our hands
tremble?

What matter if we become stubborn and stupid, unable to see the shapes of
new visions, for we shall pass?

What tragedy it would be if mankind were never to be better than we, if the
promise of the human venture were to be fastened and limited in us.

What tragedy it would be if men were to be limited to our feeble imaginings,
to our perverse clinging to superstitions and darkness.

Rather let this be our song, that new life in a springtime freshet will cause
sons and daughters, like the green grass of the fields, to come up and
cover the scarred face of the earth.

For unto us are children born; unto us new chances given, generation upon
generation.

from A Thanksgiving for Children
KENNETH L. PATTON

72

Erika

A child is a person in himself, but also the man who shall be. An uncreatured one whose life is bounded by the sensations he feels, the warmth and food he is given, and most important, by the love with which he is surrounded.

A child is man in potential, the flower whose unfolding takes place under the careful tutelage and shelter of love.

And upon each of us, parents, sponsors, teachers, rest the obligation for this love. Love freely, wisely, that the child may grow strong and straight into creative maturity. Love freely, love wisely, that the child may grow happily into manhood or womanhood. Love freely, love wisely, that the child may become. That the child may help himself fulfill himself. That the child may be all that lies within him. That the child may, in the life that lies ahead, be at peace with all that he is. Love with understanding, knowing that within each child are you and I and all humanity.

RUDOLPH W. NEMSER

Rohn Engh

It is innocence that is full and experience that is empty.
It is innocence that wins and experience that loses.

It is innocence that is young and experience that is old.
It is innocence that grows and experience that wanes.

It is innocence that is born and experience that dies.
It is innocence that knows and experience that does not know.

It is the child who is full and the man who is empty,
Empty as an empty gourd and as an empty barrel:

That is what I do with that experience of yours.

Now then, children go to school.
And you men, go to the school of life.

Go and learn
How to unlearn.

from Innocence and Experience
CHARLES PÉGUY

Between the innocence of babyhood and the dignity of manhood we find a delightful creature called a boy. Boys come in assorted sizes, weights, and colors, but all boys have the same creed: To enjoy every second of every minute of every hour of every day and to protest with noise (their only weapon) when their last minute is finished and the adult males pack them off to bed at night.

Boys are found everywhere — on top of, underneath, inside of, climbing on, swinging from, running around, or jumping to. Mothers love them, little girls hate them, older sisters and brothers tolerate them, adults ignore them, and Heaven protects them. A boy is Truth with dirt on its face, Beauty with a cut on its finger, Wisdom with bubble gum in its hair, and the Hope of the future with a frog in its pocket.

When you are busy, a boy is an inconsiderate, bothersome, intruding jangle of noise. When you want him to make a good impression, his brain turns to jelly or else he becomes a savage, sadistic jungle creature bent on destroying the world and himself with it.

A boy is a composite — he has the appetite of a horse, the digestion of a sword swallower, the energy of a pocket-size atomic bomb, the curiosity of a cat, the lungs of a dictator, the imagination of a Paul Bunyan, the shyness of a violet, the audacity of a steel trap, the enthusiasm of a fire cracker, and when he makes something he has five thumbs on each hand.

He likes ice cream, knives, saws, Christmas, comic books, the boy across the street, woods, water (in its natural habitat), large animals, Dad, trains, Saturday mornings, and fire engines. He is not much for Sunday School, company, schools, books without pictures, music lessons, neckties, barbers, girls, overcoats, adults, or bedtime.

Nobody else is so early to rise, or so late to supper. Nobody else gets so much fun out of trees, dogs, and breezes. Nobody else can cram into one pocket a rusty knife, a half-eaten apple, three feet of string, an empty Bull Durham sack, two gum drops, six cents, a slingshot, a chunk of unknown substance, and a genuine supersonic code ring with a secret compartment.

from ''What Is a Boy?''
ALAN BECK

74

Give your children your permission to grow up, to make their own lives for themselves independent of you, and independent also of your particular desires and ambitions. Give them a sense of truth; make them aware of themselves as citizens of a dangerous universe, a universe in which there are many obstacles as well as fulfillments, and prepare them for human nature in all of its varieties and forms and variabilities. Show them that they must anticipate in their lifetime pitfalls and snares and fickleness on the part of human beings from whom they could expect faithfulness. Do not make the mistake of giving your children a picture of the world that is painted in unrealistic colors in which there are lights but no shadows. Give your children a sense of proportion in the landscape of the world, a sense of the reality of life with its lights and shadows, of human nature with its goodness and its evils.

JOSHUA LOTH LIEBMAN

Nor pride of place, nor triumph of the pen
Can bring again to your repentant hand
The vanished child you failed to understand.

from "The Child"
SILENCE BUCK BELLOWS

Berne Greene

There was a time when I was very small,
  When my whole frame was but an ell in height;
Sweetly, as I recall it, tears do fall,
  And therefore I recall it with delight.

I sported in my tender mother's arms,
  And rode a-horse-back on best father's knee;
Alike were sorrows, passions, and alarms,
  And gold, and Greek, and love, unknown to me.

Then seemed to me this world far less in size,
  Likewise it seemed to me less wicked far;
Like points in heaven, I saw the stars arise,
  And longed for wings that I might catch a star.

I saw the moon behind the island fade,
  And thought, "O, were I on that island there,
I could find out of what the moon is made,
  Find out how large it is, how round, how fair!"

from "Childhood"
JENS BAGGESON

76

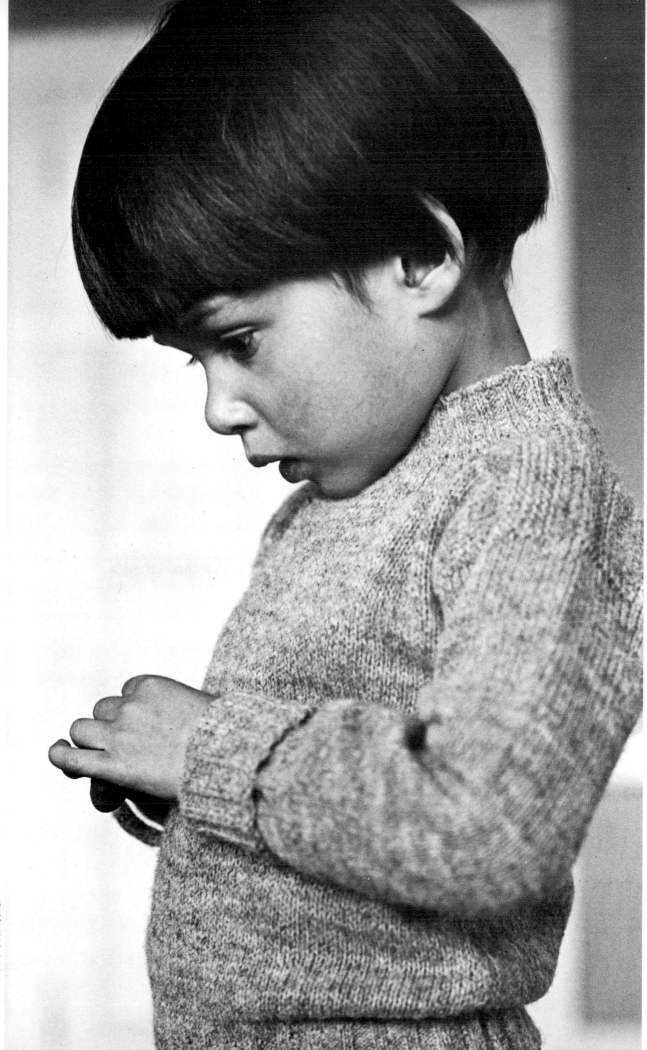

Let not young souls be smothered out before
They do quaint deeds and fully flaunt their pride.
It is the world's one crime its babes grow dull,
Its poor are ox-like, limp and leaden-eyed.
Not that they starve, but starve so dreamlessly;
Not that they sow, but that they seldom reap;
Not that they serve, but have no gods to serve;
Not that they die, but that they die like sheep.

"The Leaden-Eyed"
VACHEL LINDSAY

Take heed of this small child of earth;
   He is great; he hath in him God most high,
Children before their fleshly birth
   Are lights alive in the blue sky.

In our light bitter world of wrong
   They come; God gives us them awhile.
His speech is in their stammering tongue,
   And his forgiveness in their smile.

Their sweet light rests upon our eyes.
   Alas! their right to joy is plain.
If they are hungry Paradise
   Weeps, and, if cold, Heaven thrills with pain.

The want that saps their sinless flower
   Speaks judgment on sin's ministers.
Man holds an angel in his power.
   Ah! deep in Heaven what thunder stirs,

When God seeks out these tender things
   Whom in the shadow where we sleep
He sends us clothed about with wings,
   And finds them ragged babes that weep!

"The Poor Children"
VICTOR HUGO

midday

The sun reaches its zenith, and the full light of midday bathes life in a golden glow . . . or so it seems to those no longer young.

To Youth itself, making the stormy crossing from the dependency of childhood to the responsibilities of adult life, the joys are far from unmitigated. The splendid highs are there, but so are cavernous lows, days and nights of acute insecurity, feelings of battling upstream against a hostile world.

These are also the years for discovery of the romantic and physical joys of love. From era to era, the emphasis may shift from one to the other aspect of this overpowering new experience, and the acceptable norms for its expression may change. But the emotion itself is timeless, though each new generation discovers love as if for the first time. Never before has anyone been so gloriously happy, nor in such desperate pain.

At this paradoxical time in life, both points of view have their own validity. This is indeed a time when the potential in life can seem infinite. The young man or woman reaches the full development of his physical being. Never again is he likely to be so strong, healthy, or beautiful as he is during the days of his youth. Never again will so many options stretch before him, or so many dreams seem capable of fulfillment.

But just because of that, he is never again likely to be so vulnerable to the bitter realities that collide with his idealism, or to feel so inadequate in countless daily confrontations. Moreover, he is faced with the need to make decisions which will set the direction for the rest of his life; and he has such a small store of experience to draw upon.

In this section, we've tried to look at Youth from as many vantage points as possible. Works selected by younger writers may not be, strictly speaking, about Youth; but, like Millay's "Renascence," they capture the essence of the varying emotions felt most strongly by the young. Older authors, looking back on youth, provide a measure of perspective that illuminates still other facets of the springtime of life.

This, then, is what it means to be young, as expressed in words and photographs by leading interpreters of the human condition.

Lovely the rose; and yet—its beauty Time deflowers:
Lovely in spring the violet—but brief its hours:
White is the lily—but fast it falls and fades away:
White is the snow—but it melts from earth where it lay:
Lovely the loveliness of youth—yet lives but a day.

THEOCRITUS

Youth is a continual intoxication; it is the fever of reason.

LA ROCHEFOUCAULD

I remember my youth and the feeling that will never come back any more
— the feeling that I could last forever, outlast the sea, the earth, and all men.

JOSEPH CONRAD

Youth is the time to go flashing from one end of the world to the other
both in mind and body; to try the manners of different nations; to hear the
chimes at midnight.

from Virginibus Puerisque
ROBERT LOUIS STEVENSON

Diana Davies/Bethel Agency

I love you; not because you understand
  That there are old, crushed dreams in me,
And not because you sense my loneliness
  And give me of your sympathy.

For you, whose eyes are soft with grief
  Can find in mine no look that's sad.
I love you, friend, because you think of me
  As someone very young and glad.

"To an Older Woman"
VIOLET ALLEYN STOREY

The stars shall fade away, the sun himself
Grow dim with age, and Nature sink in years;
But thou shalt flourish in Immortal Youth.

JOSEPH ADDISON

You hear Youth laughing down green, budded aisles,
You glimpse her dancing limbs, her hair of gold,
The carefree, sweet defiance of her smiles,
For you are old.

But I can see her eyes, gray with alarm,
Misty with longings that can find no tongue,
The hooded future, clutching at her arm,
For I am young.

"Youth"
THERESA HELBURN

Rohn Engh

Do you remember, once we took together
That curving road upon the hill's ascent?
And walked much farther than we ever meant.
(So brave with sun we were, and winey weather!)
And being young, and much in love, we found
A thousand trivial things for our delay,
As hand in hand went blithely on our way,
Till suddenly the twilight closed around

And dusk came down. One small and hesitant star
Followed a slender moon across the sky—
Ah, dear my love, how swift such moments are,
That half-light interval as day goes by;
How brief a while the heart is undistressed
By the long shadows leaning from the west!

"Interval Before Night"
SARA HENDERSON HAY

I never really understood before—
    But I see now that you were very wise,
Who laughed on a brave day and closed the door
    On laughter and young living and gay skies:

Your lady was all-perfect, and your friend,
    Why, he would die for you, as you for him!
How did you know that Truth could have an end
    And Love grow querulous, and Friendship dim?

We knew all wisdom then, all wrong and right,
    The world was ours, with only Youth to pay;
And yours was more than all, O you so bright!
    But while the flame was wild you turned away;

So in that Heaven of which your songs were sung
    Earth seems a Heaven to you, remembering—
Ah, you were very wise, to be so young,
    Who closed the door, remembering only Spring.

"For a Young Man Who Died"
MARGARET WIDDEMER

Youth is easily deceived, because it is quick to hope.

from The Rhetoric
ARISTOTLE

Young blood doth not obey an old decree.

from Love's Labor's Lost, IV
WILLIAM SHAKESPEARE

How beautiful is youth! how bright it gleams
With its illusions, aspirations, dreams!
Book of beginnings, story without end,
Each maid a heroine, and each man a friend!

from ''Morituri Salutamus''
HENRY WADSWORTH LONGFELLOW

Bliss was it in that dawn to be alive,
But to be young was very Heaven.

from ''The Prelude''
WILLIAM WORDSWORTH

In youth, we clothe ourselves with rainbows and
go as brave as the zodiac.

from ''The Conduct of Life''
RALPH WALDO EMERSON

Not yet old enough for a man, nor young enough
for a boy; as a squash is before 'tis a peas-cod, or a
codling when 'tis almost an apple.

from Twelfth Night, I
WILLIAM SHAKESPEARE

Just at the age 'twixt boy and youth,
When thought is speech, and speech is truth.

from ''Marmion,'' II
SIR WALTER SCOTT

Berne Greene

89

Clemens Kalischer

In the morning of our days, when the senses are unworn and tender, when the whole man is awake in every part, and the gloss of novelty is fresh upon all the objects that surround us, how lively at that time are our sensations, but how false and inaccurate the judgments we form of things!

EDMUND BURKE

Youth no less becomes the light and careless livery that it wears, than settled age his sables and his weeds, importing health and graveness.

WILLIAM SHAKESPEARE

Unless a tree has borne blossoms in spring, you will vainly look for fruit on it in autumn.

AUGUST W. HARE

It is not easy to surround life with any circumstances in which youth will not be delightful; and I am afraid that, whether married or unmarried, we shall find the vesture of terrestrial existence more heavy and cumbrous the longer it is worn.

SIR RICHARD STEELE

The golden age never leaves the world; it exists still, and shall exist, till love, health, and poetry are no more — but only for the young.

EDWARD GEORGE BULWER-LYTTON

Youth, enthusiasm, and tenderness are like the days of spring. Instead of complaining, oh, my heart, of their brief duration, try to enjoy them.

FREDERIC RUCKERT

Ed Eckstein/Bethel Agency

At almost every step in life we meet with young men from whom we anticipate wonderful things, but of whom, after careful inquiry, we never hear another word. Like certain chintzes, calicoes, and ginghams, they show finely on their first newness, but cannot stand the sun and rain, and assume a very sober aspect after washing-day.

NATHANIEL HAWTHORNE

In the species with which we are best acquainted, namely, our own, I am far, even as an observer of human life, from thinking that youth is its happiest season, much less the only happy one.

WILLIAM PALEY

Youth is not the age of pleasure; we then expect too much, and we are therefore exposed to daily disappointments and mortifications. When we are a little older, and have brought down our wishes to our experience, then we become calm and begin to enjoy ourselves.

LORD LIVERPOOL

Like virgin parchment, capable of any inscription.

PHILIP MASSINGER

Oh, the joy of young ideas painted on the mind, in the warm, glowing colors fancy spreads on objects not yet known, when all is new and all is lovely!

HANNAH MORE

Lilo Raymond/Bethel Agency

You need repent none of your youthful vagaries. They may have been over the score on one side, just as those of age are probably over the score on the other. But they had a point; they not only befitted your age and expressed its attitude and passion but they had a relation to what was outside of you, and implied criticisms on the existing state of things, which you need not allow to have been undeserved, because you now see that they were partial. All error, not merely verbal, is a strong way of stating that the current truth is incomplete. The follies of youth have a basis in sound reason, just as much as the embarrassing questions put by babes and sucklings. Their most anti-social acts indicate the defects of our society. When the torrent sweeps the man against a boulder, you must expect him to scream, and you need not be surprised if the scream is sometimes a theory. Shelley, chafing at the Church of England, discovered the cure of all evils in universal atheism. Generous lads irritated at the injustices of society, see nothing for it but the abolishment of everything and Kingdom Come of anarchy. Shelley was a young fool; so are these cock-sparrow revolutionaries. But it is better to be a fool than to be dead. It is better to emit a scream in the shape of a theory than to be entirely insensible to the jars and incongruities of life and take everything as it comes in a forlorn stupidity. Some people swallow the universe like a pill; they travel on through the world, like smiling images pushed from behind. For God's sake give me the young man who has brains enough to make a fool of himself! As for the others, the irony of facts shall take it out of their hands, and make fools of them in downright earnest, ere the farce be over.

from Virginibus Puerisque
ROBERT LOUIS STEVENSON

94

Erika

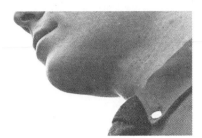

Clemens Kalischer

Do not pity the young.
Look, if the day allows,
At the light upon their brows.
Salute them passing us by,
The quick, the strict, the strong
Who will never wait, or die.
Sooner than we can say,
The young will have their way;
And have us, too, and be told
That none who live to be old
Have time to pity the young.

from "Do Not Pity the Young"
JOHN HOLMES

Miriamne: How can I help you?
Mio: You have.
Miriamne: If I were a little older — if I knew
   the things to say! I can only put out my hands
   and give you back the faith you bring to me
   by being what you are. Because to me
   you are all hope and beauty and brightness drawn
   across what's black and mean!

from "Winterset"
MAXWELL ANDERSON

When Duty whispers low, "Thou must,"
The youth replies, "I can."

RALPH WALDO EMERSON

   In America, the young are always ready to give to those who are older than themselves the full benefits of their inexperience.

OSCAR WILDE

   When we are young, we think not only ourselves, but that all about us, are immortal.

BENJAMIN DISRAELI

Berne Greene

Youth is the gay and pleasant spring of life, when joy is stirring in the dancing blood, and nature calls us with a thousand songs to share her general feast. *Not just youth...*

JOSEPH RIDGEWAY

Youth is the opportunity to do something and to become somebody.

THEODORE T. MUNGER

Youth is the period of building up in habits, and hopes, and faiths. — Not an hour but is trembling with destinies; not a moment, once passed, of which the appointed work can ever be done again, or the neglected blow struck on the cold iron.

JOHN RUSKIN

Youth is the season of hope, enterprise, and energy, to a nation as well as an individual.

WILLIAM R. WILLIAMS

Bestow thy youth so that thou mayest have comfort to remember it when it hath forsaken thee, and not sigh and grieve at the account thereof. While thou art young thou wilt think it will never have an end; but the longest day hath its evening, and thou shalt enjoy it but once; it never turns again; use it therefore as the spring-time, which soon departeth, and wherein thou oughtest to plant and sow all provisions for a long and happy life.

SIR WALTER RALEIGH

98

Algimantas Kezys, S.J.

Milwaukee Journal

Tell me what are the prevailing sentiments that occupy the minds of your young men, and I will tell you what is to be the character of the next generation.

EDMUND BURKE

Consider what heavy responsibility lies upon you in your youth, to determine, among realities, by what you will be delighted, and, among imaginations, by whose you will be led.

JOHN RUSKIN

Young men are as apt to think themselves wise enough, as drunken men are to think themselves sober enough. They look upon spirit to be a much better thing than experience, which they call coldness. They are but half mistaken; for though spirit without experience is dangerous, experience without spirit is languid and ineffective.

PHILIP DORMER STANHOPE,
4th Earl of Chesterfield

The strength and safety of a community consist in the virtue and intelligence of its youth, especially of its young men.

JOEL HAWES

Remember the days gone by

Youth is beautiful. Its friendship
is precious. The intercourse with it
is a purifying release from the worn
and stained hardness of older life.
NATHANIEL PARKER WILLIS

When I was one-and-twenty
  I heard a wise man say,
"Give crowns and pounds and guineas
  But not your heart away;
Give pearls away and rubies
  But keep your fancy free."
But I was one-and-twenty,
  No use to talk to me.

When I was one-and-twenty
  I heard him say again,
"The heart out of the bosom
  Was never given in vain;
'Tis paid with sighs a-plenty
  And sold for endless rue."
And I am two-and-twenty,
  And oh, 'tis true, 'tis true.
                "When I Was One-and-Twenty"
                A.E. HOUSMAN

Erika

It's little I care what path I take,
    And where it leads it's little I care;
But out of this house, lest my heart break,
    I must go, and off somewhere.

It's little I know what's in my heart,
    What's in my mind it's little I know,
But there's that in me must up and start,
    And it's little I care where my feet go.

I wish I could walk for a day and a night,
    And find me at dawn in a desolate place
With never the rut of a road in sight,
    Nor the roof of a house, nor the eyes of a face.

I wish I could walk till my blood should spout,
    And drop me, never to stir again,
On a shore that is wide, for the tide is out,
    And the weedy rocks are bare to the rain.

But dump or dock, where the path I take
    Brings up, it's little enough I care;
And it's little I'd mind the fuss they'll make,
    Huddled dead in a ditch somewhere.

"Is something the matter, dear," she said.
    "That you sit at work so silently?"
"No, mother, no, 'twas a knot in my thread.
    There goes the kettle, I'll make the tea."

"Departure"
EDNA ST. VINCENT MILLAY

Loveliest of trees, the cherry now
Is hung with bloom along the bough,
And stands about the woodland ride
Wearing white for Eastertide.

Now, of my threescore years and ten,
Twenty will not come again,
And take from seventy springs a score,
It only leaves me fifty more.

And since to look at things in bloom
Fifty springs are little room,
About the woodlands I will go
To see the cherry hung with snow.

"Loveliest of Trees"
A.E. HOUSMAN

Clemens Kalischer

These are the days of our youth, our days of glory and honor.
    Pleasure begotten of strength is ours, the sword in our hand.
Wisdom bends to our will, we lead captivity captive,
    Kings of our lives and love, receiving gifts from men.

       . . . .

These are the days of our youth, the days of our dominion.
    All the rest is a dream of death and a doubtful thing.
Here we at least have lived, for love is all life's wisdom,
    Joy of joys for an hour to-day; then away, farewell!

from "The Days of Our Youth"
from the Arabic
(tr. Wilfred Scawen Blunt)

When all the world is young, lad,
  And all the trees are green;
And every goose a swan, lad,
  And every lass a queen;
Then hey for boot and horse, lad,
  And round the world away;
Young blood must have its course, lad,
  And every dog his day.

CHARLES KINGSLEY

Rejoice, O young man, in thy youth; and let thy heart cheer thee in the days of thy youth, and walk in the ways of thine heart.

ECCLESIASTES XI, 9

Young men are fitter to invent than to judge, fitter for execution than for counsel, and fitter for new projects than for settled business.

from Essays, VIII
FRANCIS BACON

Your young men shall dream dreams; your old men shall see visions.

JOEL II, 28

Berne Greene

Out of the noise of tired people working,
   Harried with thoughts of war and lists of dead,
His beauty met me like a fresh wind blowing,
   Clean boyish beauty and high-held head.
Eyes that told secrets, lips that would not tell them,
   Fearless and shy the young unwearied eyes—
Men die by millions now, because God blunders,
   Yet to have made this boy he must be wise.

"A Boy"
SARA TEASDALE

Grown-up people reconcile themselves too willingly to preparing young ones for the time when they will regard as illusion what now is an inspiration to heart and mind. Deeper experience of life, however, advises their inexperience differently. It exhorts them to hold fast, their whole life through, to the thoughts which inspire them. It is through the idealism of youth that man catches sight of truth, and in that idealism he possesses a wealth which he must never exchange for anything else.

We must all be prepared to find that life tries to take from us our belief in the good and the true, and our enthusiasm for them, but we need not surrender them. That ideals, when they are brought into contact with reality, are usually crushed by facts does not mean that they are bound from the very beginning to capitulate to the facts, but merely that our ideals are not strong enough; and they are not strong enough because they are not pure and strong and stable enough in themselves.

from Memoirs of Childhood and Youth
ALBERT SCHWEITZER

D. Corry/De Wys, Inc.

Often I think of the beautiful town
    That is seated by the sea;
Often in thought go up and down
The pleasant streets of that dear old town,
    And my youth comes back to me.
        And a verse of a Lapland song
        Is haunting my memory still:
        "A boy's will is the wind's will,
And the thoughts of youth are long, long thoughts."

One of my favorite poems

from "My Lost Youth"
HENRY WADSWORTH LONGFELLOW

Lee Foster

Michael Meadows/Editorial Photocolor Archives, Inc.

A maiden modest as is she,
   So full of sweetness and forbearance,
Must be all right; her folks must be
   Delightful parents.

Her arms and face I can commend,
   And, as the writer of a poem,
I fain would compliment, old friend,
   The limbs below 'em.

Nay, be not jealous. Stop your fears.
   My tendencies are far from sporty.
Besides, the number of my years
   Is over forty.

from "Ad Kanthiam Phoceum"
QUINTUS HORATIUS FLACCUS

Erika

Gather ye rosebuds while ye may,
  Old Time is still a-flying;
And this same flower that smiles to-day,
  To-morrow will be dying.

The glorious lamp of heaven, the sun,
  The higher he's a-getting,
The sooner will his race be run,
  And nearer he's to setting.

That age is best which is the first,
  When youth and blood are warmer;
But being spent, the worse and worst
  Times still succeed the former.

Then be not coy, but use your time,
  And while ye may, go marry;
For, having lost but once your prime,
  You may forever tarry.

          "To the Virgins to Make Much of Time"
          ROBERT HERRICK

When I shall be divorced, some ten years hence,
From this poor present self which I am now;
When youth has done its tedious vain expense
Of passions that for ever ebb and flow;
Shall I not joy youth's heats are left behind,
And breathe more happy in an even clime?
Ah no! for then I shall begin to find
A thousand virtues in this hated time.
Then I shall wish its agitations back,
And all its thwarting currents of desire;
Then I shall praise the heat which then I lack,
And call this hurrying fever, generous fire,
And sigh that one thing only has been lent
To youth and age in common — discontent.

"Youth's Agitations"
MATTHEW ARNOLD

Youth is a wave, rolling away in all directions,
Part of it to break against rocks, or die on the beaches,
Or in the great calms—
And yet, the wave itself must rush on, foaming, far
   out into the distance,
Into the darkness . . .
And the next wave,
And the next,
Forever rising, forever breaking . . .

from "To a Young Friend"
ROBERT NATHAN

Clemans Kalischer

111

afternoon

Clemens Kalischer

For years, the young person has been flailing out at life, shouting ''Let me take my place in the world! I'm not a child any longer; let me make my own decisions, be responsible for my own destiny!''

There comes a time for most of us when life says ''O.K., friend; you asked for it.'' And we have entered the middle years, the afternoon of life.

Most of us fake it pretty well. To younger people coming along behind us, we appear to have things relatively under control. We are the doers, the shapers, the controllers. We oil the wheels of industry, buy and sell, plan and carry out. These are the productive years, the years of creating and raising a family, securing a place in the scheme of things, accumulating whatever power and possessions we are destined to have.

But the bare fact about the middle years, the fact that no youngster can understand, is this: in the core of our being, we never do quite make it to full adulthood. We wait for the day when we will be as all-powerful in our own small world as we knew our parents to be; but it doesn't happen. The world is fully capable of overpowering us, and we know it, however much we may achieve.

Perhaps that is why there is an undercurrent of insecurity in the middle years that surfaces in disturbing ways at crisis points along the way. When a parent dies, for instance, we are suddenly aware that we are now the responsible generation; there is no higher court of last resort. Every one looks to us to maintain the order of things; and secretly we know how tenuous is the thread by which we do so.

Small wonder, then, that the gradually accumulating evidences of our own mortality . . . the indications that we are no longer young, and will someday be old . . . take their emotional toll, even among those acknowledged to be in ''the prime of life.''

This paradox of the middle years is the subject, examined from numerous viewpoints by a variety of authors. This is life's afternoon: its bright sunshine, and its lengthening shadows.

I must have passed the crest a while ago
   And now I am going down—
Strange to have crossed the crest and not to know,
   But the brambles were always catching the hem of my gown.

All the morning I thought how proud I should be
   To stand there straight as a queen,
Wrapped in the wind and the sun with the world under me—
   But the air was dull, there was little I could have seen.

It was nearly level along the beaten track
   And the brambles caught in my gown—
But it's no use now to think of turning back,
   The rest of the way will be only going down.

"The Long Hill"
SARA TEASDALE

Clemens Kalischer

What we are usually invited to contemplate as ''ripeness'' in a man is the resigning of ourselves to an almost exclusive use of the reason. One acquires it by copying others and getting rid, one by one, of the thoughts and convictions which were dear in the days of one's youth. We believed once in the victory of truth; but we do not now. We believed in our fellow men; we do not now. We were capable of enthusiasm; but no longer. To get through the shoals and storms of life more easily we have lightened our craft, throwing overboard what we thought could be easily spared. But it was really our stock of food and drink of which we deprived ourselves; our craft is now easier to manage, but we ourselves are in a decline.

I listened in my youth, to conversations between grown-up people through which there breathed a tone of sorrowful regret which oppressed the heart. The speakers looked back at the idealism and capacity for enthusiasm of their youth as something precious to which they ought to have held fast, and yet at the same time they regarded it as almost a law of nature that no one should be able to do so. This woke in me a dread of having ever, even once, to look back on my own past with such a feeling; I resolved never to let myself become subject to this tragic domination of mere reason, and what I thus vowed in almost boyish defiance I have tried to carry out.

from Memoirs of Childhood and Youth
ALBERT SCHWEITZER

Grow up as soon as you can. It pays. The only time you really live fully is from thirty to sixty. . . . The young are slaves to dreams; the old servants of regrets. Only the middle-aged have all their five senses in the keeping of their wits.

from Anthony Adverse
HERVEY ALLEN

115

Perhaps middle age is, or should be, a period of shedding shells; the shell of ambition, the shell of material accumulations and possessions, the shell of the ego. Perhaps one can shed at this stage in life as one sheds in beach-living; one's pride, one's false ambitions, one's mask, one's armor. Was that armor not put on to protect one from the competitive world! If one ceases to compete, does one need it? Perhaps one can at last in middle age, if not earlier, be completely oneself. And what a liberation that would be!

It is true that the adventures of youth are less open to us. Most of us cannot, at this point, start a new career or raise a new family. Many of the physical, material, and worldly ambitions are less attainable than they were twenty years ago. But is this not often a relief? "I no longer worry about being the belle of Newport," a beautiful woman, who had become a talented artist, once said to me. And I always liked that Virginia Woolf hero who meets middle age admitting: "Things have dropped from me. I have outlived certain desires . . . I am not so gifted as at one time seemed likely. Certain things lie beyond my scope. I shall never understand the harder problems of philosophy. Rome is the limit of my travelling . . . I shall never see savages in Tahiti spearing fish by the light of a blazing cresset, or a lion spring in the jungle, or a naked man eating raw flesh . . ." (Thank God! you can hear him adding under his breath.)

The primitive, physical, functional pattern of the morning of life, the active years before forty or fifty, is outlived. But there is still the afternoon opening up, which one can spend not in the feverish pace of the morning but in having time at last for those intellectual, cultural, and spiritual activities that were pushed aside in the heat of the race. We Americans, with our terrific emphasis on youth, action, and material success, certainly tend to belittle the afternoon of life and even to pretend it never comes. We push the clock back and try to prolong the morning, overreaching and overstraining ourselves in the unnatural effort. We do not succeed, of course. We cannot compete with our sons and daughters. And what a struggle it is to race with these overactive and under-wise adults! In our breathless attempts we often miss the flowering that waits for afternoon.

For is it not possible that middle age can be looked upon as a period of second flowering, second growth, even a kind of second adolescence? It is true that society in general does not help one accept this interpretation of the second half of life. And therefore this period of expanding is often tragically misunderstood. Many people never climb above the plateau of forty-to-fifty. The signs that presage growth, so similar, it seems to me, to those in early adolescence: discontent, restlessness, doubt, despair, longing, are interpreted falsely as signs of decay. In youth one does not as often misinterpret the signs; one accepts them, quite rightly, as growing pains. One takes them seriously, listens to them, follows where they lead. One is afraid. Naturally. Who is not afraid of pure space — that breath-taking empty space of an open door? But despite fear, one goes through to the room beyond.

But in middle age, because of the false assumption that it is a period of decline, one interprets these life-signs, paradoxically, as signs of approaching death. Instead of facing them, one runs away; one escapes — into depressions, nervous breakdowns, drink, love affairs, or frantic, thoughtless, fruitless overwork. Anything, rather than face them. Anything, rather than stand still and learn from them. One tries to cure the signs of growth, to exorcise them, as if they were devils, when really they might be angels of annunciation.

Erika

Elihu Blotnick/B.B.M. Associates

Angels of annunciation of what? Of a new stage in living when, having ✳ shed many of the physical struggles, the worldly ambitions, the material encumbrances of active life, one might be free to fulfill the neglected side of one's self. One might be free for growth of mind, heart, and talent; free at last for spiritual growth; free of the clamping sunrise shell. Beautiful as it was, it was still a closed world one had to outgrow.

from Gift From The Sea
ANNE MORROW LINDBERGH

Suddenly in the dusk I heard them cry,
The gray geese veering south
In the gray sky;
And halted, finger on mouth,
Knowing that summer was past and the brave year sped
Pinion to taut-stretched pinion, overhead.
Wherefore, I said:
"This is the autumn—turn to the warm blaze now,
To the window latched, and the sturdy door made fast,
To the firm drawn blind.
This is the hour for lamps, and the student brow
Bent over books; this is the time to keep
Logs for the hearth, and fagots for the mind,
And a bed for winter sleep—"

Heart in the listening breast, are you as wise?
The season passes. What were the wings we heard
Beating the dark air, faint in the windy skies,
What southward wheeling bird?

"The Gray Geese Fly"
SARA HENDERSON HAY

118

In our youth-oriented society, childhood gets a lot of loving attention, old age is viewed with terror — and middle age is simply ignored. There isn't even an accepted specific noun for a person in this last age group; *middle-ager*, the only one listed in the unabridged Webster's, is a word you seldom hear used in ordinary conversation.

from The Middle-Age Crisis
BARBARA FRIED

Now, uniquely, man can see the whole of life's time while still in its midst, looking back as he could not do when he was young, and forward as he will not do when very old. His perspective is 360 degrees. It enables discovery of optimum use of time.

from The New Years: A New Middle Age
ANNE W. SIMON

'Tis a maxim with me to be young as long as one can: there is nothing can pay one for that invaluable ignorance which is the companion of youth; those sanguine groundless hopes, and that lively vanity, which make all the happiness of life. To my extreme mortification I grow wiser every day.

LADY MARY WORTLEY MONTAGU

Nancy Flowers/Bethel Agency

When I see birches bend to left and
right
Across the line of straighter darker
trees,
I like to think some boy's been
swinging them.
But swinging doesn't bend them
down to stay.
Ice storms do that. Often you must
have seen them
Loaded with ice a sunny winter
morning
After a rain. They click upon themselves
As the breeze rises, and turn many-
colored
As the stir cracks and crazes their
enamel.
Soon the sun's warmth makes them
shed crystal shells
Shattering and avalanching on the
snow crust —
Such heaps of broken glass to sweep
away
You'd think the inner dome of heav-
en had fallen.
They are dragged to the withered
bracken by the load,
And they seem not to break; though,
once they are bowed
So low for long, they never right
themselves:
You may see their trunks arching in
the woods
Years afterward, trailing their leaves
on the ground
Like girls on hands and knees that
throw their hair
Before them over their heads to dry
in the sun.
But I was going to say when Truth
broke in
With all her matter of fact about the
ice storm
(Now am I free to be poetical?)
I should prefer to have some boy
bend them
As he went out and in to fetch the
cows —
Some boy too far from town to learn
baseball,
Whose only play was what he found
himself,
Summer or winter, and could play
alone.
One by one he subdued his father's
trees
By riding them down over and over
again
Until he took the stiffness out of
them,
And not one but hung limp, not one
was left
For him to conquer. He learned all
there was
To learn about not launching out too
soon
And so not carrying the tree away
Clear to the ground. He always kept
his poise
To the top branches, climbing care-
fully
With the same pains you use to fill a
cup
Up to the brim, and even above the
brim.
Then he flung outward, feet first,
with a swish,
Kicking his way down through the
air to the ground.
So was I once myself a swinger of
birches;
And so I dream of going back to be.
It's when I'm weary of consid-
erations,
And life is too much like a pathless
wood
Where your face burns and tickles
with cobwebs
Broken across it, and one eye is
weeping
From a twig's having lashed across it
open.
I'd like to get away from earth
awhile
And then come back to it and begin
over.
May no fate willfully misunderstand
me
And half grant what I wish and
snatch me away
Not to return. Earth's the right place
for love:
I don't know where it's likely to go
better.
I'd like to go by climbing a birch
tree,

120

And climb black branches up a
   snow-white trunk
Toward heaven, till the tree could
   bear no more,
But dipped its top and set me down
   again.
That would be good both going and
   coming back.
One could do worse than be a
   swinger of birches.

"Birches"
ROBERT FROST

121

It is still hard for me, remembering
   That I have gone three-quarters of the way—
The wind still feels like Spring,
   And every day another flowering day:

Tomorrow will be running past my lawn
   With something quite as wonderful to find,
And every colored dawn
   The same surprise as those I've left behind —

I know — each closing flower and closing sun
   Brings me more close to my own evening —
But maybe, when all's done
   I'll open a last gate, and still find Spring.

"Bright Journey"
MARGARET WIDDEMER

A man who at twenty is a young Lothario, for example, and at thirty a dashing young man about town, at forty becomes, without having changed his personality or habits one iota, a roué who very soon will qualify for the ultimate distinction of being a dirty old man.

from The Middle-Age Crisis
BARBARA FRIED

Well, who wants to be young, anyhow, any idiot born in the last forty years
    can be young, and besides forty-five isn't really old, it's right on the
    border;
At least, unless the elevator's out of order.

OGDEN NASH

Venus, again thou mov'st a war
   Long intermitted, pray thee, pray thee spare!
I am not such, as in the reign
   Of the good Cynara I was; refrain
Sour mother of sweet Loves, forbear
   To bend a man, now at his fiftieth year.

from "To Venus"
QUINTUS HORATIUS FLACCUS

And indeed there will be time
For the yellow smoke that slides along the street,
Rubbing its back upon the window-panes;
There will be time, there will be time
To prepare a face to meet the faces that you meet;
There will be time to murder and create,
And time for all the works and days of hands
That lift and drop a question on your plate;
Time for you and time for me,
And time yet for a hundred indecisions,
And for a hundred visions and revisions,
Before the taking of a toast and tea.

In the room the women come and go
Talking of Michelangelo.

And indeed there will be time
To wonder, "Do I dare?" and, "Do I dare?"
Time to turn back and descend the stair,
With a bald spot in the middle of my hair—
(They will say: "How his hair is growing thin!")
My morning coat, my collar mounting firmly to the
    chin,
My necktie rich and modest, but asserted by a simple
    pin—
(They will say: "But how his arms and legs are
    thin!")
Do I dare
Disturb the universe?
In a minute there is time
For decisions and revisions which a minute will
    reverse.

For I have known them all already, known them all:
Have known the evenings, mornings, afternoons,

I have measured out my life with coffee spoons;
I know the voices dying with a dying fall
Beneath the music from a farther room.
    So how should I presume?

And I have known the eyes already, known them
    all—
The eyes that fix you in a formulated phrase.
And when I am formulated, sprawling on a pin,
When I am pinned and wriggling on the wall,
Then how should I begin
To spit out all the butt ends of my days and ways?
    And how should I presume?

            . . . .

And the afternoon, the evening, sleeps so peacefully!
Smoothed by long fingers,
Asleep . . . tired . . . or it malingers,
Stretched on the floor, here beside you and me.
Should I, after tea and cakes and ices,
Have the strength to force the moment to its crisis?
But though I have wept and fasted, wept and prayed,
Though I have seen my head (grown slightly bald)
    brought in upon a platter
I am no prophet—and here's no great matter;
I have seen the moment of my greatness flicker,
And I have seen the eternal Footman hold my coat,
    and snicker,
And in short, I was afraid.

from "The Love Song of J. Alfred Prufrock"
T.S. ELIOT

Nancy Flowers/Bethel Agency

Something beautiful from Canada...

I've looked at love from both sides now
From give and take, and still somehow
It's love's illusions I recall
I really don't know love at all

Tears and fears and feeling proud
To say "I love you" right out loud
Dreams and schemes and circus crowds
I've looked at life that way

But now old friends are acting strange
They shake their heads, they say I've changed
But something's lost, but something's gained
In living ev'ry day

I've looked at life from both sides now
From win and lose and still somehow
It's life's illusions I recall
I really don't know life at all....

from "Both Sides, Now"
JONI MITCHELL

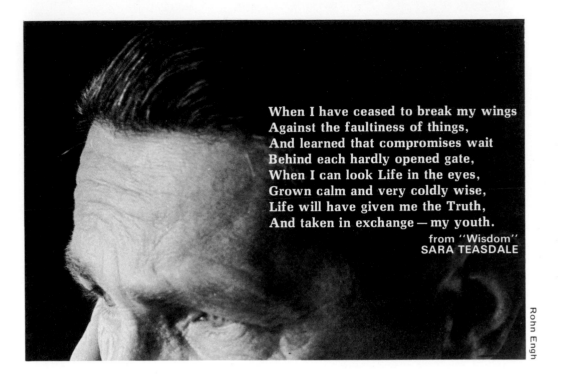

When I have ceased to break my wings
Against the faultiness of things,
And learned that compromises wait
Behind each hardly opened gate,
When I can look Life in the eyes,
Grown calm and very coldly wise,
Life will have given me the Truth,
And taken in exchange — my youth.

from "Wisdom"
SARA TEASDALE

Rohn Engh

The Adult from 38 to 45

Forty is a noticeably restless, introspective, morose, moody, peevish, and melancholy person. Thirty is sunny, cheerful, hard-working, and obedient to the demands of daily routines. Forty, in comparison, is dilatory, rebellious, and dawdles over necessary tasks, and when he is chided for his negligence, he tends to respond with sullen and belligerent defiance. When asked to describe his life, Forty will reply vaguely that it is "awful," "boring," "dull," or "depressing," without being able to say exactly why. Thirty is satisfied with familiar surroundings and content to play with his own toys. Not so Forty, who instead is continually on the lookout for greener pastures and who spends much time daydreaming about running away with someone who will really appreciate him. Forty tends to be morbidly convinced that he is actually very sick (brain cancer and heart trouble are two especially favored self-diagnoses), and to grieve over the degeneration, both real and imagined, of his physical and mental capacities. It is not too much to say that Forty manages to make life miserable for those who must live with him, possibly because he seems unable to live with himself. Genuinely loving solicitude cannot satisfy repeated, unreasonable, and often tear-filled protestations about being unloved and neglected. Temper tantrums also occur in this age group with distressing frequency, and it is unfortunate but true that disciplinary action usually results merely in making things worse, not better.

from The Middle-Age Crisis
BARBARA FRIED

We stand for a moment, like those who pause upon a mountain path, and gaze downward to the valley they have left below and upward to the heights above that allure to further effort. We have been brought to our present point by powers we know not of, but whether our feet shall ever stand upon those high and lonely levels depends upon ourselves.

We are like voyagers when the harbor dangers have been safely passed, the pilot dropped, and the ship heads out to sea. From now on, the voyage is our own: ours the task of making it a joy; ours to prepare to weather the unfeeling, destructive storm; ours to find in the pageantry of Nature and in comradeship with our fellows a sufficient inspiration.

from Words of Aspiration
ARTHUR WAKEFIELD STATEN

It is when his mental powers are already beginning to decline that a man is capable of the greatest works; just as it is hotter in July, and at two o'clock in the afternoon, when the sun has turned and is on the downward grade, than it is in June at midday.

GEORGE C. LICHTENBERG

At fifty a man's real life begins. He has acquired upon which to achieve; received from which to give; learned from which to teach; cleared upon which to build.

E.W. BOK

We are, God Help us, mature women in a world measured by a teenager's waist.

from "June in Limbo"
MARYA MANNES

Grow up as soon as you can. It pays. The only time you really live fully is from thirty to sixty.

HERVEY ALLEN

✳ The boy gathers materials for a temple, and then when he is thirty concludes to build a woodshed.

HENRY DAVID THOREAU

I was standing in the snow by my car when I realized that meaning had fled my life.

from The Seeker
ALLEN WHEELIS

With steady foot and even pace
I tread the Milky Way;
I've youth without its levity
And age without decay.

from A Review of the Affairs of
France and All Europe, VIII
DANIEL DEFOE

✳ Until 30 I lived in a magic world. It was . . . the acquisition of knowledge, or rather of information of every kind. After 30 I began very slowly to want not only to be informed, but to understand. It is the problem with which I have been occupied ever since.

from Sunset and Twilight
BERNARD BERENSON

Thomas A. Brown, Jr.

130

One of the things that makes Forty seem so much like Fourteen, then, is just that he, too, is trying to decide what life "means" in relation, usually almost exclusively, to "who" he "is." Where Forty and Fourteen differ of course is that this is the second time around for the adult: what he is involved in is not so much a quest for identity as an inquest. His identity conflicts express the fact that he is overhauling, from his middle-aged vantage point, precisely that series of social and personal commitments that he chose to give meaning to his life twenty-odd years before. While the teenager is trying desperately to decide, "Who am I? What shall I do? Where shall I go? Whom shall I love?" his father (or mother), who may be somewhat quieter about it without being any the less desperate, is mumbling, "What am I doing here? What have I done? And now how the hell am I going to manage to get out of it?" Or, as one unhappy Forty said, "Sure, I feel trapped. Why shouldn't I? Twenty-five years ago a dopey eighteen-year-old college kid made up **his** mind that **I** was going to be a dentist. So now here I am, a dentist. I'm stuck. What I want to know is, who told that kid he could decide what I was going to have to do for the rest of my life?"

from The Middle-Age Crisis
BARBARA FRIED

You give your cheeks a rosy stain,
 With washes dye your hair,
But paint and washes both are vain
 To give a youthful air.

Those wrinkles mock your daily toil;
 No labor will efface them;

You wear a mask of smoothest oil,
 Yet still with ease we trace them.

An art so fruitless then forsake,
 Which though you much excel in,
You never can contrive to make
 Old Hecuba young Helen.

"Artificial Beauty"
LUCIANUS

The middle-age crisis is ubiquitous. Unlike other crises — physical, familial, financial, social — which are generally individual affairs, this one is shared by all of us. Each of us goes through it in his own way, experiences it with greater or lesser intensity, and emerges from it more or less reconciled to the years ahead. It is a "natural" developmental crisis, and it is unavoidable.

. . . .

To enter middle age is to cross a threshold into an unknown world. It is exciting for some, a source of apprehensiveness for others. If we resolve this transitional period by immersing ourselves in the past or by stewing in the hostility that is stimulated by frustration and conflict, we make a stagnant choice. It is obviously far better to seek constructive and forward-looking solutions. The loss of youth and physical prowess is more than offset by the status, power, authority and wide experience that the middle-aged person enjoys in our society.

from Introduction to The Middle-Age Crisis
MORRIS I. STEIN

Erika

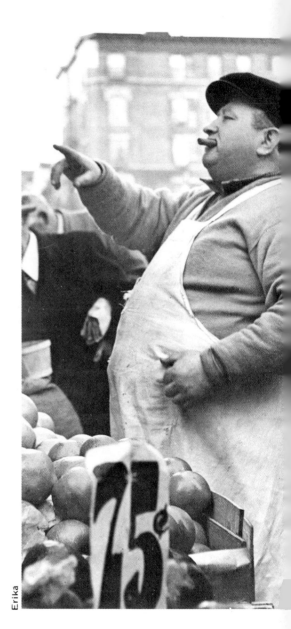

Erika

It was a night of early spring,
  The winter-sleep was scarcely broken;
Around us shadows and the wind
  Listened for what was never spoken.

Though half a score of years are gone,
  Spring comes as sharply now as then—
But if we had it all to do
  It would be done the same again.

It was a spring that never came;
  But we have lived enough to know
That what we never have, remains;
  It is the things we have that go.

from "Wisdom"
SARA TEASDALE

When all the fiercer passions cease
  (The glory and disgrace of youth);
When the deluded soul, in peace,
  Can listen to the voice of truth;
When we are taught in whom to trust,
  And how to spare, to spend, to give,
(Our prudence kind, our pity just,)
  'Tis then we rightly learn to live.

"Reflections"
GEORGE CRABBE

On his bold visage, middle age
Had slightly press'd its signet sage,
Yet had not quenched the open truth
And fiery vehemence of youth;
Forward and frolic glee was there,
The will to do, the soul to dare.

from "The Lady of the Lake," I
SIR WALTER SCOTT

What is to come we know not. But we know
That what has been was good — was good to show,
Better to hide, and best of all to bear.
We are the masters of the days that were:
We have lived, we have loved, we have suffered — even so.

Shall we not take the ebb who had the flow?
Life was our friend. Now, if it be our foe —
Dear, though it spoil and break us! — need we care
What is to come?

"Bric-A-Brac"
W.E. HENLEY

137

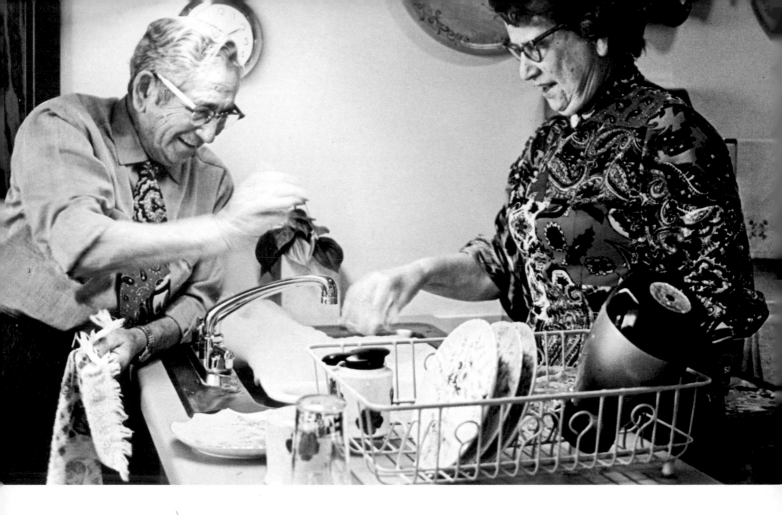

*   For real true love, love at first sight, love to devotion, love that robs a man of his sleep, love that "will gaze an eagle blind," love that "will hear the lowest sound when the suspicious tread of theft is stopped," love that is "like a Hercules, still climbing trees in the Hespirides," — we believe the best age is from forty-five to seventy; up to that, men are generally given to mere flirting.

ANTHONY TROLLOPE

And finally, to be honest, most of us would have to admit that at our age we make rotten star-crossed lovers, anyway. We've lived too long to be able to be absolute, we've made too many mistakes to be judgmental, and we are aware that even passion, that most humorless of emotions, can be ridiculous. Suppose for a moment that Romeo's father and Juliet's mother had met at that ball and fallen in love with each other at first sight. It's easy to imagine that they might be swept with desire for one another, just as their children were. It's not so easy to see them mismanaging their affair so that they end up killing themselves by mistake for love. They would know better. All Forties know better. It's only adolescents who are able to believe there's no tomorrow and die accordingly; their parents have learned from experience that tomorrow always comes and so does the morning after. They may use the excitement of falling in love again to help them temporarily forget this regrettable fact, but it doesn't really change things. The sun calmly continues to rise, and we are all, in love or not, a day older — and that much closer to Darby and Joan.

from The Middle-Age Crisis
BARBARA FRIED

138

One by one, like leaves from a tree,
All my faiths have forsaken me;
But the stars above my head
Burn in white and delicate red,
And beneath my feet the earth
Brings the sturdy grass to birth.
I who was content to be
But a silken-singing tree,
But a rustle of delight
In the wistful heart of night—

I have lost the leaves that knew
Touch of rain and weight of dew.
Blinded by a leafy crown
I looked neither up nor down—
But the little leaves that die
Have left me room to see the sky;
Now for the first time I know
Stars above and earth below.

"Leaves"
SARA TEASDALE

When you came, you were like red wine and honey,
And the taste of you burnt my mouth with its sweetness.
Now you are like morning bread,
Smooth and pleasant.
I hardly taste you at all, for I know your savor;
But I am completely nourished.

"A Decade"
AMY LOWELL

Berne Greene

The days grow shorter,
The nights grow longer,
The headstones thicken along the way;
And life grows sadder,
But love grows stronger
For those who walk with us day by day.

ELLA WHEELER WILCOX

   Young love is a flame; very pretty, often very hot and fierce, but still only
light and flickering. The love of the older and disciplined heart is as coals,
deep-burning, unquenchable.

HENRY WARD BEECHER

Middle age is the time when a man
is always thinking that in a week or
two he will feel as good as ever.

from "The Almost Perfect State"
DON MARQUIS

Shades of the prison-house begin to close
  Upon the growing Boy,
But he beholds the light, and whence it flows,
  He sees it in his joy;
The Youth, who daily farther from the east
  Must travel, still is Nature's Priest,
  And by the vision splendid
  Is on his way attended;
At length the Man perceives it die away,
And fade into the light of common day.

from "Intimations of Immortality"
WILLIAM WORDSWORTH

Yet Ah, that Spring should vanish with
    the Rose!
That Youth's sweet-scented manuscript
    should close!
  The Nightingale that in the branches sang,
Ah whence, and whither flown again,
    who knows!

from "The Rubáiyát"
OMAR KHAYYÁM
(tr. Edward Fitzgerald)

S. Furushima

Erika

To put it bluntly, the one-fifth of the population that is between forty and sixty is obliged to carry the weight for the other four-fifths. No other group is as well fitted for this task as they, who are wiser than the young, stronger than the old, and freer than either; and society simply ratifies their expertise, endurance, and independence when it invests more real and symbolic power in them than in any other age group. Middle-agers call the tune: not only because they pay the piper, which they can well afford to do since they earn more money than anybody else, but also because they have written and really know the score.

from The Middle-Age Crisis
BARBARA FRIED

Too often, too true, my friend! But not for us, I believe. I believe you + I have learned how to live + love each moment of our lives

She sat down again with her heart just nowhere, and took up the table-cloth, but for a long time she couldn't see the stitches. She was wondering what had become of her life; every day she had thought something great was going to happen, and it was all just straying from one terrible disappointment to another. Here in the lamplight sat Dennis and the cats, beyond in the darkness and snow lay Winston and New York and Boston, and beyond that were far off places full of life and gayety she'd never seen nor even heard of, and beyond everything like a green field with morning sun on it lay youth and Ireland as if they were something she had dreamed, or made up in a story. Ah, what was there to remember, or to look forward to now?

from "The Cracked Looking Glass"
KATHERINE ANNE PORTER

With a gigantic upheaval, twentieth-century America has created a time of life which no other civilization has known. At middle age, now in truth the middle of adult years, a halfway mark instead of a kindly euphemism for the beginning of the end, most people can count on as many years to live as have been lived since they were twenty-one. The years ahead are no more static nor monolithic than those which have gone before. Change, fast and profound, has in a few decades split the solid block of old years and carved out a new time of life, an opportunity without precedence.

from The New Years: A New Middle Age
ANNE W. SIMON

Olivier Rebbot/Bethel Agency

143

She had eyes of deepest brown
And her hair was all a-curl
In gentle hands she held my heart
Though she was such a little girl.

I was all the world to her,
Beautiful and good and wise.
I was honesty and truth,
Mirrored in a baby's eyes.

Suddenly I'm old and dull,
A barrier to all that's gay.
When did those adoring eyes
Faltering, slowly look away?

Now she dreams her dreams apart.
Once she told them all to me.
I, who'd give my life for her,
Have become The Enemy.

She was such a little girl,
Only yesterday, I vow.
When did her hand slip from mine?
Will I never find her now?

"The Enemy"
ETHEL BOEHM FOTH

Gone are the games of childhood,
    And gone forever is youth,
And gone is the world that was kind to us,
    And love, and faith, and truth.

from "Mein Kind, Wir Waren Kinder"
HEINRICH HEINE

There's little in taking or giving,
    There's little in water or wine;
This living, this living, this living
    Was never a project of mine.
Oh, hard is the struggle, and sparse is
    The gain of the one at the top,
And art is a form of catharsis,
    And love is a permanent flop,
And work is the province of cattle,
    And rest's for a clam in a shell,
So I'm thinking of throwing the battle —
    Would you kindly direct me to hell?

"Coda"
DOROTHY PARKER

Olivier Rebbot/Bethel Agency

144

I am all alone in the room,
The evening stretches before me
Like a road all delicate gloom
Till it reaches the midnight's gate.
And I hear his step on the path,
And his questioning whistle, low
At the door as I hurry to meet him.

He will ask, "Are the doors all
    locked?
Is the fire made safe on the hearth?
And she—is she sound asleep?"

I shall say, "Yes, the doors are
    locked,
And the ashes are white as the frost:
Only a few red eyes
To stare at the empty room.
And she is all sound asleep,
Up there where the silence sings,
And the curtains stir in the cold."

He will ask, "And what did you do
While I have been gone so long?
So long! Four hours or five!"

I shall say, "There was nothing I
    did —
I mended that sleeve of your coat.
And I made her a little white hood
Of the furry pieces I found
Up in the garret today.
She shall wear it to play in the snow,
Like a little white bear—and shall
    laugh,
And tumble, and crystals of stars
Shall shine on her cheeks and hair.
It was nothing I did—I thought
You would never come home again!"

Then he will laugh out, low,
Being fond of my folly. Perhaps;
And softly and hand in hand
We shall creep upstairs in the dusk
To look at her, lying asleep:
Our little gold bird in her nest:
The wonderful bird who flew in
At the window our life flung wide.
(How should we have chosen her,
Had we seen them all in a row,
The unborn vague little souls,
All wings and tremulous hands?
How should we have chosen her,
Made like a star to shine,
Made like a bird to fly,
Out of a drop of our blood,
And earth, and fire, and God?)

The we shall go to sleep,
Glad—
   Oh God, did you know
When you molded men out of clay,
Urging them up and up
Through the endless circles of
   change,
Travail and turmoil and death,
Many would curse you down,
Many would live all gray
With their faces flat like a mask:
But there would be some, O God,
Crying to you each night,
"I am so glad! So glad!
How shall I thank you, God?"

Was that one thing you knew
When you smiled and found it was
   good:
The curious teeming earth
That grew like a child at your hand?
Ah, you might smile, for that!—

—I am all alone in the room.
The books and the pictures peer,
Dumb old friends from the dark.
The wind goes high on the hills,
And my fire leaps out, being proud.
The terrier, down on the hearth,
Twitches and barks in his sleep,
Soft little foolish barks,
More like a dream than a dog . . .
I will mend the sleeve of that coat,
All ragged,—and make her the hood
Furry, and white, for the snow.
She shall tumble and laugh . . .
   Oh, I think
Though a thousand rivers of grief
Flood over my head—though a hill
of horror lie on my breast,—
Something will sing, "Be glad!
You have had all your hearts desire:
The unknown things that you asked
When you lay awake in the nights,
Alone, and searching the dark
For the secret wonder of life.
You have had them (Can you for-
   get?):
The ancient beautiful things!"

How long he is gone. And yet
It is only an hour or two. . . .
Oh, I am so happy. My eyes
Are troubled with tears.
   Did you know,
O God, they would be like this,
Your ancient beautiful things?
Are there more? Are there
   more, — out there? —
O God, are there always more?

"The Ancient Beautiful Things"
FANNIE STEARNS DAVIS

147

I am done with the years that were; I am quits;
  I am done with the dead and the old.
They are mines worked out; I delved in their pits;
  I have saved their grain of gold.

Now I turn to the future for wine and bread;
  I have bidden the past adieu.
I laugh and lift hands to the years ahead:
  ''Come on! I am ready for you!''

''The Look Ahead''
EDWIN MARKHAM

evening

Algimantas Kezys, S. J.

Herb Taylor/Editorial Photocolor Archives, Inc.

The day draws near its close; and the whole of life assumes some measure of perspective.

Has it been a magnificent adventure, or an exercise in futility? Is it crowned in serenity, or are we left alone in the dark as the powers of our full maturity diminish? Are we, in old age, substantially different than we were in youth . . . or are we still the children we once were, a little bewildered to find our bodies and our worlds so changed that we can hardly recognize them?

Has death become an enemy to be fought and feared, or a kind friend leading us to peace, and to a joyous reunion with those we have loved?

Even those who are still in the morning of their years must wonder sometimes what it will be like to be approaching the end of all that we have known.

Poets and writers through the centuries have pondered the mysteries of life's evening hours. Some have seen old age as the rich fulfillment of life, some as a mocking emptiness, sustained only by memories of a happier time. Listen to their voices, exploring what it means to grow old.

Some have left
and others are about to leave;
so why should we be sorry
that we too must go?
And yet our hearts are sad
that on this mighty road
the friends we meet can set
no place to meet again.

           from the Sanskrit
           (tr. Daniel Ingalls)

Now voyager, lay here your dazzled head.
Come back to earth from air, be nourished,
Not with that light on light, but with this bread.

Here close to earth be cherished, mortal heart,
Hold your way deep as roots push rocks apart
To bring the spurt of green up from the dark.

Where music thundered let the mind be still,
Where the will triumphed let there be no will,
What light, revealed, now let the dark fulfill.

Here close to earth the deeper pulse is stirred,
Here where no wings rush and no sudden bird,
But only heart-beat upon beat is heard.

Here let the fiery burden be all spilled,
The passionate voice at last be calmed and stilled
And the long yearning of the blood fulfilled.

Now voyager, come home, come home to rest,
Here on the long-lost country of earth's breast
Lay down the fiery vision, and be blest, be blest.

           "Now Voyager"
           MAY SARTON

Max Tharpe

How strange it seems, with so much gone
Of life and love, to still live on.

from ''Snow-Bound''
JOHN GREENLEAF WHITTIER

Youth longs and manhood strives, but
  age remembers,
Sits by the raked-up ashes of the past,
Spreads its thin hands above the whit-
  ening embers
That warm its creeping life-blood to
  the last.

from ''The Iron Gate''
OLIVER WENDELL HOLMES

The grandeur and exquisiteness of old age.

from ''Song at Sunset''
WALT WHITMAN

The days darken round me, and the years,
Among new men, strange faces, other minds.

from Morte d'Arthur
SIR THOMAS MALORY

I'm growing fonder of my staff;
  I'm growing dimmer in the eyes;
I'm growing fainter in my laugh;
  I'm growing deeper in my sighs;
I'm growing careless of my dress;
  I'm growing frugal of my gold;
I'm growing wise; I'm growing — yes —
  I'm growing old.

from ''I'm Growing Old''
J.G. SAXE

It is not the end of joy that makes old age so sad, but the end of hope.

from Titan XXXII
JEAN PAUL RICHTER

We do not count a man's years, until he has nothing else to count.

RALPH WALDO EMERSON

152

Berne Greene

Do not go gentle into that good night,
Old age should burn and rave at close of day;
Rage, rage against the dying of the light.

Though wise men at their end know dark is right,
Because their words had forked no lightning they
Do not go gentle into that good night.

Good men, the last wave by, crying how bright
Their frail deeds might have danced in a green bay,
Rage, rage against the dying of the light.

Wild men who caught and sang the sun in flight,
And learn, too late, they grieved it on its way,
Do not go gentle into that good night.

Grave men, near death, who see with blinding sight
Blind eyes could blaze like meteors and be gay,
Rage, rage against the dying of the light.

And you, my father, there on the sad height,
Curse, bless, me now with your fierce tears, I pray.
Do not go gentle into that good night.
Rage, rage against the dying of the light.

"Do Not Go Gentle into That Good Night"
DYLAN THOMAS

153

I am not resigned to the shutting away of loving hearts in the hard ground.
So it is, and so it will be, for so it has been, time out of mind:
Into the darkness they go, the wise and the lovely. Crowned
With lilies and with laurel they go; but I am not resigned.

Lovers and thinkers, into the earth with you.
Be one with the dull, the indiscriminate dust.
A fragment of what you felt, of what you knew,
A formula, a phrase remains, — but the best is lost.
. . . .
Down, down, down into the darkness of the grave
Gently they go, the beautiful, the tender, the kind;
Quietly they go, the intelligent, the witty, the brave.
I know. But I do not approve. And I am not resigned.

from ''Dirge Without Music''
EDNA ST. VINCENT MILLAY

Old Eben Flood, climbing alone one night
Over the hill between the town below
And the forsaken upland hermitage
That held as much as he should ever know
On earth again of home, paused warily.
The road was his with not a native near;
And Eben, having leisure, said aloud,
For no man else in Tilbury Town to hear:

"Well, Mr. Flood, we have the harvest moon
Again, and we may not have many more.
The bird is on the wing, the poet says,
And you and I have said it here before.
Drink to the bird." He raised up to the light
The jug that he had gone so far to fill.
And answered huskily, "Well, Mr. Flood,
Since you propose it, I believe I will."

       . . . .

Then, as a mother lays her sleeping child
Down tenderly, fearing it may awake,
He set the jug down slowly at his feet
With trembling care, knowing that most things break;
And only when assured that on firm earth
It stood, as the uncertain lives of men
Assuredly did not, he paced away,
And with his hand extended paused again:

"Well, Mr. Flood, we have not met like this
In a long time; and many a change has come
To both of us, I fear, since last it was
We had a drop together. Welcome home!"
Convivially returning with himself,
Again he raised the jug up to the light;
And with an acquiescent quaver said:
"Well, Mr. Flood, if you insist, I might."

Only a very little, Mr. Flood —
For auld lang syne. No more, sir; that will do!"
So, for the time, apparently it did,
And Eben evidently thought so too;
For soon amid the silver loneliness
Of night he lifted up his voice and sang,
Secure, with only two moons listening,
Until the whole harmonious landscape rang —

"For auld lang syne." The weary throat gave out,
The last word wavered: and the song being done,
He raised again the jug regretfully
And shook his head, and was again alone.
There was not much that was ahead of him,
And there was nothing in the town below —
Where strangers would have shut the many doors
That many friends had opened long ago.

from "Mr. Flood's Party"
EDWIN ARLINGTON ROBINSON

Give me your hand
By these grey waters —
The day is ending.

Already the first
Faint star pierces
The veil of heaven.

Oh, the long way
We two have come,
In joy, together,

To these grey shores
And quiet waters
And the day's ending!

The day is ending.
The journey is ended.
Give me your hand.

"Telos"
JOHN HALL WHEELOCK

Berne Greene

People expect old men to die,
They do not really mourn old men.
Old men are different. People look
At them with eyes that wonder when . . .
People watch with unshocked eyes . . .
But the old men know when an old man dies.

"Old Men"
OGDEN NASH

Max Tharpe

The good man talked to her of high and holy things —
He left her mind a tumult of trumpets, crowns, and wings —
He talked to her of Heaven — and all she saw the while
Were two arms waiting and an unforgotten smile
And a neat white cottage with lilacs by the door
And the blue plates shining and the sun across the floor
And an old clock ticking the happy hour to come
When the little gate opened and her man came home.
When she gets to Heaven, there is nothing she will miss —
When she finds her Heaven, it will be like this.

"Sermon in an Almshouse"
THEODOSIA GARRISON

157

Bruce Anspach/Editorial Photocolor Archives, Inc.

I shall not run upstairs again,
   And oh, the foolish grief I feel
I must go carefully or pain
   Will thrust me through with its bright steel.

I never thought that I should care
   When the first shadow fell on me.
I planned lace caps for my white hair
   And hoped to grow old gracefully.

I thought that when age came I'd stand
   (If age should really come at all!)
And greet him with extended hand
   As my last partner at a ball.

But now when you with easy grace
   Run up ahead or wait for me,
Such bitterness is in my face
   I turn my head lest you should see.

"Candles that Burn"
ALINE KILMER

Max Tharpe

✳ It gives me great pleasure to converse with the aged. They have been over the road that all of us must travel, and know where it is rough and difficult and where it is level and easy.

from The Republic
PLATO

Old age has a great sense of calm and freedom. When the passions have relaxed their hold you have escaped, not from one master, but from many.

from The Republic
PLATO

* I think perhaps after all
That I should like to be old.
I will paint little lacquered boxes then
With orange birds
(No one will be doing it anymore.)
They will say — "Orange! How hideous!
They were done that way in her day."
And I shall nod benignly, and go on painting —
Painting pleasant futile orange birds for a present
To my young self, who had no time, because she had
    to be living.

I will read and make emphatic judgments on old essays
And write little new ones, chiseling them
Very long, very meticulously, because then time
    won't count,
And nobody need read them after they are done,
So why hurry?

I shall sentimentalize over my old friends and lovers
Very tenderly, very satisfyingly, because they will mostly
    be dead;
I shall wrap myself in how we loved each other,
Omitting how we failed each other,
Because I shall know then that even such things as that
    didn't matter;

Only the delicate painting of orange birds,
And the delicate shaping of trivial perfect essays —
For time will not be a thing to use then,
But to get rid of.

The young people, tiptoeing round me
Will pretend to me that I matter,
And that the world still takes seriously what I do.
They will be kind, I think, So I shall not let them know
That I know I do not matter, and like the painlessness of it:
Nor even how wonderful it is
To be able to paint orange birds that nobody wants
On little tin tea boxes that I have lacquered black,
And to carve little ivory essays
About forgotten arguments and people,
Laughing to myself complacently over my own demoded
    humor . . .

I wish I were painting futile, long-tailed orange birds
On little black tin tea boxes.

"Orange Birds"
MARGARET WIDDEMER

Waning years steal from us our pleasures one
    by one; they have already snatched away
    my jokes, my loves, my revellings, and my play.

from Epistles II
HORACE

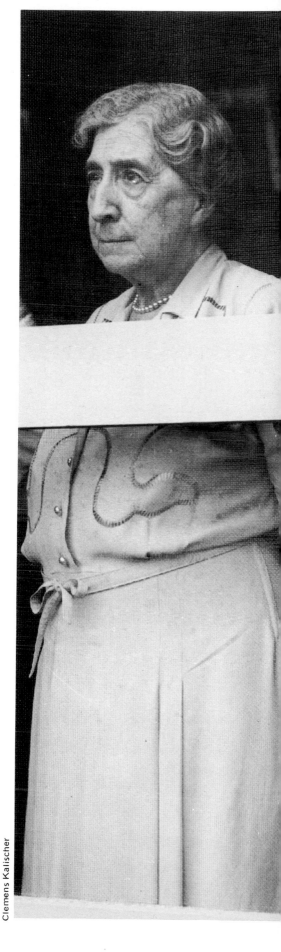

Clemens Kalischer

One capital advantage of old age is the absolute insignificance of a success more or less. I went to town and read a lecture yesterday. Thirty years ago it had really been a matter of importance to me whether it was good and effective. Now it is of none in relation to me. It is long already fixed what I can do and what I cannot do.

RALPH WALDO EMERSON

Old age brings along with its ugliness the comfort that you will soon be out of it. . . . To be out of the war, out of debt, out of the drouth, out of the blues, out of the dentist's hands, out of the second thoughts, mortifications, and remorses that inflict such twinges and shooting pains — out of the next winter, and the high prices, and the company below your ambition....

RALPH WALDO EMERSON

The tragedy of old age is not that one is old, but that one is young.

OSCAR WILDE

And now we are aged and gray, Maggie,
And the trials of life nearly done;
Let us sing of the days that are gone, Maggie,
When you and I were young.

from ''When You and I Were Young, Maggie''
GEORGE W. JOHNSON

I shall have winter now and lessening days,
Lit by a smoky sun with slanting rays,
And after falling leaves, the first determined frost.
The colors of the world will all be lost.
So be it; the faint buzzing of the snow
Will fill the empty boughs,
And after sleet storms I shall wake to see
A glittering glassy plume of every tree.
Nothing shall tempt me from my fire-lit house.
And I shall find at night a friendly ember
And make my life of what I can remember.

"Winter"
SARA TEASDALE

For the unlearned, old age is winter;
for the learned, it is the season of the harvest.
HASIDIC SAYING

Each part of life has its own pleasures. Each has its own abundant harvest, to be garnered in season. We may grow old in body, but we need never grow old in mind and spirit. We must make a stand against old age. We must atone for its faults by activity. We must exercise the mind as we exercise the body, to keep it supple and buoyant. Life may be short, but it is long enough to live honorably and well. Old age is the consummation of life, rich in blessings.

CICERO

Winter is on my head, but spring is in my heart.

VICTOR HUGO

To me, old age is always fifteen years older than I am.

BERNARD BARUCH

Nancy Flowers/Bethel Agency

Lilo Raymond/Bethel Agency

Grow old along with me!
The best is yet to be,
The last of life, for which the first
    was made;
Our times are in his hand
Who saith, ''A whole I planned,
Youth shows but half. Trust God; see
    all, nor be afraid!''

ROBERT BROWNING

My age is as a lusty Winter
Frosty, but kindly.

from As You Like It
WILLIAM SHAKESPEARE

The riders in a race do not stop short when they reach the goal. There is a little finishing canter before coming to a standstill. There is time to hear the kind voice of friends and to say to one's self: ''The work is done.''

from a speech on his 91st birthday
OLIVER WENDELL HOLMES II

Clemens Kalischer

Clemens Kalischer

Be with me, Beauty, for the fire is dying;
My dog and I are old, too old for roving.
Man, whose young passion sets the spindrift flying,
Is soon too lame to march, too cold for loving.
I take the book and gather to the fire,
Turning old yellow leaves; minute by minute
The clock ticks to my heart. A withered wire,
Moves a thin ghost of music in the spinet.
I cannot sail your seas, I cannot wander
Your cornland, nor your hill-land, nor your valleys
Ever again, nor share the battle yonder
Where the young knight the broken squadron rallies.
Only stay quiet while my mind remembers
The beauty of fire from the beauty of embers.

from ''On Growing Old''
JOHN MASEFIELD

Old and alone sit we,
Caged, riddle-rid men,
Lost to earth's ''Listen!'' and ''See!''
Thought's ''Wherefore?'' and ''When?''
Only far memories stray
Of a past once lovely, but now
Wasted and faded away,
Like green leaves from the bough.
Vast broods the silence of night;
And the ruinous moon
Lifts on our faces her light,
Whence all dreaming is gone.
We speak not; trembles each head;
In their sockets our eyes are still;
Desire as cold as the dead,
Without wonder or will.

''The Old Men''
WALTER DE LA MARE

In a little while I will be gone from you, my people, and whither I cannot tell. From nowhere we come, into nowhere we go. What is life? It is the flash of a firefly in the night. It is the breath of a buffalo in the wintertime. It is the shadow that runs across the grass and loses itself in the sunset.

CHIEF CROWFOOT

There is a wicked inclination in most people to suppose an old man decayed in his intellect. If a young or middle-aged man, when leaving a company, does not recollect where he laid his hat, it is nothing; but if the same inattention is discovered in an old man, people will shrug up their shoulders, and say, "His memory is going."

SAMUEL JOHNSON

Vengeful across the cold November moors,
Loud with ancestral shame there came the bleak
Sad wind that shrieked, and answered with a shriek,
Reverberant through lonely corridors.
The old man heard it; and he heard, perforce,
Words out of lips that were no more to speak —
Words of the past that shook the old man's cheek
Like dead, remembered footsteps on old floors.

And then there were the leaves that plagued him so!
The brown, thin leaves that on the stones outside
Skipped with a freezing whisper. Now and then
They stopped, and stayed there — just to let him know
How dead they were; but if the old man cried,
They fluttered off like withered souls of men.

"The Pity of the Leaves"
EDWIN ARLINGTON ROBINSON

165

Abide with me, fast falls the eventide;
The darkness deepens, Lord with me abide;
When other helpers fail and comforts flee,
Help of the helpless, O abide with me.

Swift to the close ebbs out life's little day;
Earth's joys grow dim, its glories pass away;
Change and decay in all around I see;
O thou who changest not, abide with me!

. . . .

Hold thou thy Cross before my closing eyes,
Shine through the gloom, and point me to the skies;
Heaven's morning breaks, and earth's vain shadows flee;
In life, in death, O Lord, abide with me.

from Abide With Me
HENRY FRANCIS LYTE

166

Clemens Kalischer

His words were magic and his heart was true,
    And everywhere he wandered he was blessed.
Out of all ancient men my childhood knew
    I choose him and I mark him for the best.
Of all authoritative liars, too,
    I crown him loveliest.

How fondly I remember the delight
    That always glorified him in the spring;
The joyous courage and the benedight
    Profusion of his faith in everything!

Max Tharpe

He was a good old man, and it was right
    That he should have his fling.

And often, underneath the apple-trees,
    When we surprised him in the summer time,
With what superb magnificence and ease
    He sinned enough to make the day sublime!
And if he liked us there about his knees,
    Truly it was no crime.

All summer long we loved him for the same
    Perennial inspiration of his lies;
And when the russet wealth of autumn came,
    There flew but fairer visions to our eyes —
Multiple, tropical, winged with a feathery flame,
    Like birds of paradise.

So to the sheltered end of many a year
    He charmed the seasons out with pageantry
Wearing upon his forehead, with no fear,
    The laurel of approved iniquity.
And every child who knew him, far or near,
    Did love him faithfully.

                    "Uncle Ananias"
            EDWIN ARLINGTON ROBINSON

May this be our song at 77!

I was seventy-seven come August,
   I shall shortly be losing my bloom;
I've experienced zephyr and raw gust
   And (Symbolic) flood and simoon.

When you come to this time of abatement,
   To this passing from summer to fall,
It is manners to issue a statement
   As to what you got out of it all.

So I'll say, though reflection unnerves me
   And pronouncements I dodge as I can
That I think (If my memory serves me)
   There was nothing more fun than a man!

In my youth, when the crescent was too wan
   To embarrass with beams from above,
By the aid of some local Don Juan
   I fell into the habit of love.

And I learned how to kiss and be merry — an
   Education left better unsung.
My neglect of the waters Pierian
   Was a scandal, when grandma was young.

Though the shabby unbalanced the splendid,
   And the bitter outmeasured the sweet,
I should certainly do as I then did,
   Were I given the chance to repeat.

For contrition is hollow and wraithful
   And regret is no part of my plan
And I think (if my memory's faithful)
   There was nothing more fun than a man!

"The Little Old Lady in Lavender Silk"
DOROTHY PARKER

Erika

168

Max Tharpe

As a white candle
  In a holy place,
So is the beauty
  Of an aged face.

As the spent radiance
  Of the winter sun,
So is a woman
  With her travail done,

Her brood gone from her,
  And her thoughts as still
As the waters
  Under a ruined mill.

"The Old Woman"
JOSEPH CAMPBELL

You are beautiful and faded,
Like an old opera tune
Played upon a harpsichord;
Or like the sun-flooded silks
Of an eighteenth-century boudoir.
In your eyes
Smolder the fallen roses of outlived minutes,
And the perfume of your soul
Is vague and suffusing,
With the pungence of sealed spice-jars.
Your half-tones delight me,
And I grow mad with gazing
At your blent colors.

My vigor is a new minted penny,
Which I cast at your feet.
Gather it up from the dust
That its sparkle may amuse you.

"A Lady"
AMY LOWELL

You can see them alongside the shuffleboard courts in Florida or on the porches of the old folks' homes up north: an old man with snow-white hair, a little hard of hearing, reading the newspaper through a magnifying glass; an old woman in a shapeless dress, her knuckles gnarled by arthritis, wearing sandals to ease her aching arches. They are holding hands, and in a little while they will totter off to take a nap, and then she will cook supper, not a very good supper, and they will watch television, each knowing exactly what the other is thinking, until it is time for bed. They may even have a good, soul-stirring argument, just to prove that they still really care. And through the night they will snore unabashedly, each resting content because the other is there. They are in love, they have always been in love, although sometimes they would have denied it. And because they have been in love they have survived everything that life could have thrown at them, even their own failures.

ERNEST HAVEMANN

Nancy Flowers/Bethel Agency

. . . There is a case for keeping wrinkles. They are the long-service stripes earned in the hard campaign of life.. . . A wrinkled face is a firm face, a steady face, a safe face. Wrinkles are the dried-up riverbeds of a lifetime's tears. Wrinkles are the nostalgic remnants of a million smiles. Wrinkles are the crannies and footholds on the smooth visage of life on which man can cling and gain some comfort and security.

from an editorial, "In Praise of Wrinkles"
LONDON DAILY MAIL

I went to the dances at Chandlerville,
And played snap-out at Winchester.
One time we changed partners
Driving home in the moonlight of middle June,
And then I found Davis.
We were married and lived together for seventy years,
Enjoying, working, raising the twelve children,
Eight of whom we lost
Ere I had reached the age of sixty.
I spun, I wove, I kept the house, I nursed the sick,
I made the garden, and for holiday
Rambled over the fields where sang the larks,
And by Spoon River gathering many a shell,
And many a flower and medicinal weed —
Shouting to the wooded hills, singing to the green valleys.
At ninety-six I had lived enough, that is all,
And passed to a sweet repose.
What is this I hear of sorrow and weariness,
Anger, discontent and drooping hopes?
Degenerate sons and daughters,
Life is too strong for you —
It takes life to love Life.

"Lucinda Matlock"
EDGAR LEE MASTERS

Clemens Kalischer

An old man in a house is a good sign.
BENJAMIN FRANKLIN

Erika

Be life what it has been, and let us hold,
Dear wife, the names we each gave each of old.
And let not time work change upon us two
I still your boy, and still my sweetheart you.
What though I outlive Nester? and what though
You in your turn a Sibyl's years should know?
Ne'er let us know old age or late or soon:
Count not the years, but take of each its boon.

"To His Wife"
DECIMUS MAGNUS AUSONIUS

God gave us our memories so that we might have roses in December.

JAMES M. BARRIE

"Good-night! Good-night!" as we so oft have said,
Beneath this roof at midnight, in the days
That are no more, and shall no more return.
Thou hast but taken up thy lamp and gone to bed;
I stay a little longer, as one stays
To cover up the embers that still burn.

HENRY WADSWORTH LONGFELLOW

Spend your brief moment according to nature's law, and serenely greet the journey's end as an olive falls when it is ripe, blessing the branch that bare it, and giving thanks to the tree that gave it life.

MARCUS AURELIUS

"How is John Quincy Adams today?" a friend asked the former president on his 81st birthday.

"Quite well, thank you," Adams replied. "John Quincy Adams is quite well. But the house in which he lives is becoming quite dilapidated. Time and the seasons have nearly destroyed it. It is tottering on its foundations and the roof is worn quite thin. Yes, the old tenement is becoming quite uninhabitable and I fear John Quincy Adams will have to move out of it quite soon. But he himself is quite well, thank you, quite well."

recalled by
REPRESENTATIVE R. YATES

Rohn Engh

Max Tharpe

"A writhled forehead, hair gone gray,
   Fallen eyebrows, eyes gone blind and red,
Their laughs and looks all fled away,
   Yea, all that smote men's hearts are fled;
   The bowed nose, fallen from goodlihead;
Foul flapping ears like water-flags;
   Peaked chin, and cheeks all waste and dead,
And lips that are two skinny rags:

"Thus endeth all the beauty of us.
   The arms made short, the hands made lean,
The shoulders bowed and ruinous,
   The breasts, alack! all fallen in;
The flanks too, like the breasts, grown thin;

   . . . .
   For the lank thighs, no thighs but skin,
They are speckled with spots like sausage-meat.

"So we make moan for the old sweet days,
   Poor old light women, two or three
Squatting above the straw-fire's blaze.
   The bosom crushed against the knee.
   Like fagots on a heap we be,
Round fires soon lit, soon quenched and done;
   And we were once so sweet, even we!
Thus fareth many and many an one."

           from "The Complaint of the Fair Armoress"
           FRANCOIS VILLON

Le temps s'en va, le temps s'en va madame!
Las! le temps non: mais "NOUS nous en allons!"

Time goes, you say? Ah, no!
Alas, Time stays, *we* go;
  Or else, were this not so,
What need to chain the hours,
For Youth were always ours?
  Time goes, you say? — ah, no!

Ours is the eyes' deceit
Of men whose flying feet
  Lead through some landscape low;
We pass, and think we see
The earth's fixed surface flee: —
  Alas, Time stays, — we go!

Once in the days of old,
Your locks were curling gold,
  And mine had shamed the crow.
Now, in the self-same stage,
We've reached the silver age;
  Time goes, you say? — ah, no!

Once, when my voice was strong,
I filled the woods with song
  To praise your "rose" and "snow";
My bird, that sang, is dead;
Where are your roses fled?
  Alas, Time stays, — we go!

See, in what traversed ways,
What backward Fate delays
  The hopes we used to know;
Where are your old desires? —
Ah, where those vanished fires?
  Time goes, you say? — ah, no!

How far, how far, O Sweet,
The past behind our feet
  Lies in the even glow!
Now on the forward way,
Let us fold hands, and pray;
  Alas, Time stays, — *we* go.

"The Paradox of Time"
PIERRE DE RONSARD

178

Here is the long-bided hour: the labor of years is accomplished.
Why should this sadness unplumbed secretly weigh on my heart?
Is it, my work being done, I stand like a laborer, useless,
One who has taken his pay, a stranger to tasks that are new?
Is it the work I regret, the silent companion of midnight,
Friend of the golden-haired Dawn, friend of the gods of the hearth?

"Work"
ALEXANDER SERGEYVICH PUSHKIN

John Anderson my jo, John,
    When we were first acquent,
Your locks were like the raven,
    Your bonie brow was brent;
But now your brow is beld, John,
    Your locks are like the snaw,
But blessings on your frosty pow,
    John Anderson my jo!

John Anderson my jo, John,
    We clamb the hill thegither,
And monie a cantie day, John,
    We've had wi' ane anither;
Now we maun totter down, John,
    And hand in hand we'll go,
And sleep thegither at the foot,
    John Anderson my jo!

"John Anderson My Jo"
ROBERT BURNS

I strove with none; for none was worth my strife.
    Nature I loved, and next to Nature, Art;
I warmed both hands before the fire of life,
    It sinks, and I am ready to depart.

"On His Seventy-Fifth Birthday"
WALTER SAVAGE LANDOR

Richard Knapp/Photo Trends

I have had playmates, I have had companions,
In my days of childhood, in my joyful school-days:
All, all are gone, the old familiar faces.

I have been laughing, I have been carousing,
Drinking late, sitting late, with my bosom cronies;
All, all are gone, the old familiar faces.

I loved a love once, fairest among women;
Closed are her doors on me, I must not see her —
All, all are gone, the old familiar faces.

I have a friend, a kinder friend has no man;
Like an ingrate, I left my friend abruptly;
Left him, to muse on the old familiar faces.

Ghost-like I paced round the haunts of my childhood.
Earth seemed a desert I was bound to traverse,
Seeking to find the old familiar faces.

Friend of my bosom, thou more than a brother,
Why wert not thou born in my father's dwelling?
So might we talk of the old familiar faces —

How some they have died, and some they have left me,
And some are taken from me; all are departed;
All, all are gone, the old familiar faces.

"The Old Familiar Faces"
CHARLES LAMB

180

The old woman sat before the window in the thin fall sunlight, watching the street which the chill autumn wind had swept clear of people. Her veined and ancient hands seemed the only part of her still alive, until now and then a passing automobile aroused a flicker of interest in her faded eyes.

But her hands were never still. Incessantly they plucked at the grey striped apron ties around her thin waist. Now they discovered a knotted bit of string in the pocket, and worked diligently at its untangling, while those apathetic eyes never moved from the deserted street.

She was not watching for anyone, this old woman. She was not even lost in dreams for, when one has seen eighty years go by, in smoke and flame, shadow and sun, the memory of those years is dim, and what is recalled seems to be a part of any life, not the special property of one. There had been children once, and a gay young husband — even, many years ago, a pioneer father, and a proud, uncomplaining mother. But all this was past, almost forgotten, except when her grandchildren begged for a story, and she roused herself long enough to recount some tale of long ago.

In the main, however, age had spread a patina over the years in kindness, since the constant memory of so many sharp sorrows, so many deep ecstasies, would have been too much for frail old age to bear. And so she sat in the scant sunlight and tried to collect her thoughts.

from ''Homecoming''
ETHEL BOEHM FOTH

How beautiful, my friend!

Bit by bit, nevertheless, it comes over us that we shall never again hear the laughter of our friend, that this one garden is forever locked against us. And at that moment begins our true mourning, which, though it may not be rending, is yet a little bitter. For nothing, in truth, can replace that companion. Old friends cannot be created out of hand. Nothing can match the treasure of common memories, of trials endured together, of quarrels and reconciliations and generous emotions. It is idle, having planted an acorn in the morning, to expect that afternoon to sit in the shade of the oak.

from Wind, Sand, and Stars
ANTOINE DE SAINT-EXUPÉRY

Aging paints every action gray, lies heavy on every movement, imprisons every thought, it governs each decision with a ruthless and single-minded perversity. To age is to learn the feeling of no longer growing; of struggling to do old tasks, to remember familiar actions. . . .

The world becomes narrower as friends and family die or move away. To climb stairs, to ride in a car, to walk to the corner, to talk on the telephone; each action seems to take away from the energy needed to stay alive. Everything is limited by the strength you hoard greedily. Your needs decrease, you require less food, less sleep, and finally less human contact; yet this little bit becomes more and more difficult. You fear that one day you will be reduced to the simple acts of breathing and taking nourishment. This is the ultimate stage you dread, the period of helplessness and hopelessness, when independence will be over.

from Nobody Ever Died of Old Age
SHARON R. CURTIN

Ken Bouche/Katherine Young

We are but older children, dear,
Who fret to find our bedtime near.

from Through the Looking Glass
LEWIS CARROLL

Black Star

George P. Koshollek Jr. / Milwaukee Journal

Death is only an old door
    Set in a garden wall.
On gentle hinges it gives, at dusk,
    When the thrushes call.

Along the lintel are green vines,
    Beyond the light lies still,
Very willing and weary feet
    Go under that sill.

There's nothing to trouble any heart
    Nothing to fear at all,
Death is only a quiet door
    In an old wall.

"Death Is a Door"
NANCY BYRD TURNER

When you are old and gray and full of sleep,
And nodding by the fire, take down this book,
And slowly read, and dream of the soft look
Your eyes had once, and of their shadows deep;

How many loved your moments of glad grace,
And loved your beauty with love false or true;
But one man loved the pilgrim soul in you,
And loved the sorrows of your changing face.

And bending down beside the glowing bars
Murmur, a little sadly, how love fled
And paced upon the mountains overhead
And hid his face amid a crowd of stars.

"When You Are Old"
WILLIAM BUTLER YEATS

Erika

epilogue: a summing up

Rowland Scherman/Bethel Agency

Life and death are brothers that dwell together; they cling to each other and cannot be separated. They are joined by the two extremes of a frail bridge over which all created beings travel. Life is the entrance; death is the exit. Life builds, death demolishes; life sows, death reaps; life plants, and death uproots.

from Duties of the Heart
BAHYA IBN PAKUDA

Max Tharpe

And so the day ends; the journey, or at least that part of it contained within earthly boundaries, is complete.

What has it all meant? We have asked many questions throughout the course of this book; there are few definitive answers. What is true may be true only for a given person, at a given point in time and space. Or it may be an eternal verity, common to all mankind.

Diverse sources have attempted a summation of the mystery of life.

Some see the individual life as a transitory thing, a fleeting moment in eternity, significant primarily for the part it plays in the continuing chain of humanity:

The creature is born, it fades away, it dies,
And comes then the great cold.
It is the great cold of night, it is the dark.

The bird comes, it flies, it dies,
And comes then the great cold.
It is the great cold of night, it is the dark.

The fish swims away, it goes, it dies,
And comes then the great cold.
It is the great cold of night, it is the dark.

Man is born, he eats and sleeps. He fades away,
And comes then the great cold.
It is the great cold of night, it is the dark.

And the sky lights up, the eyes are closed,
The star shines.
The cold down here, the light up there.

Man is gone, the prisoner is freed,
The shadow has disappeared.
The shadow has disappeared.

PYGMY FUNERAL HYMN
(tr. Rex. Benedict)

186

Death is sweet when it comes in its time and in its place, when it is part of the order of things. For a mother death is only half a death. Each life in turn bursts like a pod and sends forth its seed. When a mother dies, for a second time the umbilical cord is cut. For a second time the knot is loosened, the knot that bound one generation to another.

And now the mother lies broken but at rest, a vein from which the gold has been extracted. In their turn, her sons and daughters will bring forth young from their mould. So simple is this image of a generation dropping one by one its white-haired members as it makes its way through time and through its metamorphoses towards a truth that is its own.

This is life that is handed on here from generation to generation with the slow progress of a tree's growth, but it is also fulfilment. What a mysterious ascension! From a little bubbling lava, from the vague pulp of a star, from a living cell miraculously fertilized, we have issued forth and have bit by bit raised ourselves to the writing of cantatas and the weighing of nebulae.

from Wind, Sand, and Stars
ANTOINE DE SAINT-EXUPÉRY

Max Tharpe

Fleeting as were the dreams of old,
Remembered like a tale that's told,
We pass away.
HENRY WADSWORTH LONGFELLOW

All things are gluttonously devoured by Time, all things are fleeting.
All things, though fixed, are flowing, nothing abides long;
Rivers grow less in their banks, the great sea-bed is uncovered,
The mountain ranges vanish and their high pinnacles fall.
Why speak of so small a thing? For even the glorious masses
Of heaven must be consumed, at last, by their own fires.
Death waits for all, and to die is a law not a punishment:
A time will come when there will be no world here.

SENECA

   Man cometh forth like a flower from concealment, and of a sudden shows himself in open day, and in a moment is by death withdrawn from open view into concealment again. The greenness of the flesh exhibits us to view, but the dryness of dust withdraws us from men's eyes. For whereas infancy is going on to childhood, childhood to youth, youth to manhood, and manhood to old age, and old age to death, in the course of the present life he is forced by the very steps of his increase upon those of decrease, and is ever wasting from the very cause whence he thinks himself to be gaining ground in the space of his life. For we cannot have a fixed stay here, whither we are come only to pass on.

GREGORY THE GREAT

One of the best

To-morrow, and to-morrow, and to-morrow,
Creeps in this petty pace from day to day,
To the last syllable of recorded time;
And all our yesterdays have lighted fools
The way to dusty death. Out, out brief candle!
Life's but a walking shadow, a poor player
That struts and frets his hour upon the stage
And then is heard no more: it is a tale
Told by an idiot, full of sound and fury,
Signifying nothing.

from Macbeth, V
WILLIAM SHAKESPEARE

190

Other writers view the changes wrought by time and circumstances as surface manifestations, not altering the basic composition of human life itself. As the sea is changeless, despite the widely varying face it shows us, so there is something eternal in man's experience, and within each individual soul. They see a deeper continuity within us all that transcends the boundaries of earthly life, and makes of death just another milestone along the way:

Life is eternal; and love is immortal; and death is only a horizon; and a horizon is nothing save the limit of our sight.

from A Commendatory Prayer
ROSSITOR WORTHINGTON RAYMOND

Some things will never change. The voice of forest water in the night, a woman's laughter in the dark, the clean, hard rattle of raked gravel, the cricketing stitch of midday in hot meadows, the delicate web of children's voices in bright air — these things will never change.

The glitter of sunlight on roughened water, the glory of the stars, the innocence of morning — these things will always be the same.

All things belonging to the earth will never change — the leaf, the blade, the flower, the wind that cries and sleeps and wakes again, the trees whose stiff arms clash and tremble in the dark — these things will always be the same, for they come up from the earth that never changes.

THOMAS WOLFE

Build thee more stately mansions, O my soul,
   As the swift seasons roll!
   Leave thy low-vaulted past!
Let each new temple, nobler than the last,
Shut thee from heaven with a dome more vast,
   Till thou at length art free,
Leaving thine outgrown shell by life's unresting sea!

from "The Chambered Nautilus"
OLIVER WENDELL HOLMES

Clemens Kalischer

Someday, when our day is ended, and our journey complete, we may find the answers to all of our questions, as Countee Cullen suggests:

Life who was not loth to trade her unto death, has done
Better than he planned, has made her wise as Solomon.
Now she knows the why and wherefore,
Troublous Whence and Whither,
Why men strive & sweat & care for
Bays that droop and wither.
All the stars she knows by name,
End and origin thereof,
Knows if love be kin to shame,
If shame be less than love.
What was crooked now is straight,
What was rough is plain;
Grief and sorrow have no weight
Now to cause her pain. . . .

from "Threnody for a Brown Girl"
COUNTEE CULLEN